TALLGRASS PRAIRIE

☐ Original tallgrass area
■ Remaining tallgrass area

■ Tallgrass
☐ Midgrass
■ Shortgrass

Tallgrass Prairie

The Inland Sea

TALLGRASS PRAIRIE
The Inland Sea

by PATRICIA D. DUNCAN

Foreword by Stewart L. Udall

THE LOWELL PRESS / KANSAS CITY

Duncan, Patricia D., 1932—
Tallgrass Prairie: The Inland Sea

Bibliography: p.
1. Prairie ecology—Kansas
2. Prairie ecology—United States
I. Title

QH105.K3D85   574.5'264   78-60177
ISBN 0-913504-44-0   ISBN 0-913504-56-4 paperback

FIRST EDITION
Second Printing, 1979

Printed in the United States of America

This book is dedicated
to my parents
Edith C. DuBose and Robert W. DuBose
and to
my husband
Herbert E. Duncan, Jr.

CONTENTS

FOREWORD BY
STEWART L. UDALL

The national park idea originated in the United States over a century ago. The essence of this concept was that a country should identify samples of the finest landscapes and preserve them untrammeled for posterity.

At the beginning of the 1960s, when a last-ditch campaign was being mounted to round out our national park system, a high priority was given to establishment of a prairie national park in a part of Kansas containing a representative remnant of the original tallgrass prairie. We wanted an area sufficiently spacious that the original ecosystem, including buffalo and other wildlife, could be restored.

Largely due to fierce local opposition and a lack of national awareness about the importance of prairie conservation, this effort was not successful. Eleven new national seashore parks were created in the 1960s, and Congress also carved out four new national parks (in California's Redwood country, in Washington's North Cascades, in the Guadalupe Mountains of Texas, and in the eroded Canyonlands of southern Utah), but the prairie park idea was thwarted, and today the great grasslands of the mid-continent constitute one of the few major land forms not included in our national system.

But conservationists are stubborn, and thanks to a few dedicated individuals the prairie park concept is still alive in 1978. Among these, no one has been more determined—or has probed deeper into the wonder and beauty of America's big grass country—than the naturalist-photographer, Patricia Duncan.

This book is a record of one person's love affair with the land—and the land's interaction with its people. Each page, each picture reminds us of the glories of an ever-changing landscape and the meaning the plains country has had to its Indians, its settlers, its wildlife.

This is, as you will soon see, much more than a book of beautiful pictures. It is a history of land use, a story of the impact of an environment on those who have lived in this unique region, and a personalized account of how a few committed individuals kept a "lost cause" from being finally lost.

Long ago America's mountains found their champion in John Muir. The sea, too, found its interpreter much later in Rachel Carson. And now, give thanks, what some have called "the inland sea" has, at last, acquired its own authentic voice in the person of Patricia Duncan. Turn the pages and you will understand why I offer this accolade—and why I am betting this book will inspire the country to demand the establishment of a national park in the Flint Hills of Kansas.

ACKNOWLEDGMENTS

It is impossible to thank everyone who has helped; and it is beyond my ability to find adequate words for those who taught me about the prairie: Raymond and Mary Hall, Larry Wagner, Ray Wagner, Charles Stough, Ivan Boyd, Lloyd Hulbert, Eugene Dehner, Ken Babcock, and Dwight Platt.

Congressman Larry Winn, Jr. of Kansas will be remembered for keeping the tallgrass prairie alive in the Congress of the United States. Linda Billings of the Sierra Club and Destry Jarvis of the National Parks and Conservation Association have given many hours to the prairie. Dr. Dick Curry of the Interior Department has been a long time friend. Charles Callison, formerly of the National Audubon Society, Mike McCloskey of the Sierra Club, and David Brower of Friends of the Earth have lent the prestige of their organizations to the cause of the prairie. Stewart Udall will go down in history as one of the greatest of all our Interior Secretaries.

Katharine Ordway has given us many prairies to hand down to future generations. Richard Pough, one of America's great conservationists, has been a constant friend and advisor. John Humke and Pat Noonan made the resources of the Nature Conservancy available to me. Dr. Karl Menninger has been an active leader and a source of inspiration. Elaine Shea has held together our citizen's organization, Save the Tallgrass Prairie, Inc., through years of selfless devotion. Brian Miller has been a tireless and creative worker. There are many others in the prairie family including Ann Bueker, Tim Amsden, Kay Wahl, Lucia Landon, Carole Hunter, and Julie Halford. I wish I could mention them all.

Lloyd Schnell of the Kansas City Art Institute introduced me to photography. David Strout helped organize the material. Kim Dooley typed the manuscript. Payson Lowell, David Spaw, Doug Petty, and Barbara Forsman of The Lowell Press had a vision of the book and encouraged me to realize the vision.

I am grateful to all the prairie people who allowed me to photograph them and record their words.

Last and most important I thank my parents who took me to the natural world very early; my husband Herb and my sons David and Don for years of patience and help and for providing a loving, peaceful, and free environment which allows my heart and mind to soar to the far reaches of all my prairies.

WHAT IS A PRAIRIE?

"We must somehow take a wider view, look at the whole landscape, really see it, and describe what's going on there."

Annie Dillard
Pilgrim at Tinker Creek

When I was six or seven years old and living in southern Arkansas, my parents took my brother and me to the high plains, the buffalo-grass-covered prairie of the Texas panhandle, to visit my grandmother, Rachel Caledonia Hunt. Rachel's parents had immigrated from Scotland to the southern states during the tortured closing days of the Civil War, and her mother had died at Rachel's birth. Rachel grew up with relatives, moved to Texas, outlived several husbands, had many children, and learned the lessons of the frontier. Rachel was a pioneer woman, a prairie woman, and she made a lasting impression on me.

At the time of our visit, Rachel told us tales of the early days, of coming to Texas in a covered wagon; but mostly I remember the table-flat land where her house stood with miles and miles of treeless space in all directions. The house itself was earth-colored boards, two or three rooms, a porch, and a fenced yard with some chickens running around. The only vegetation was a few hollyhocks blooming above the worn, bare ground. The house seemed part of the earth, as did grandmother, lying on a bed just inside the front door. I remember her crackly voice and her face, sun browned and as weather lined as the prairie dirt outside. Rachel's favorite trick, when she had our attention, was to take out her glass eye and plop it in a cup beside the bed.

So, grandmother introduced me to the prairie. I never forgot her face, her voice, her house, and, most of all, her wide-open landscape. These memories would surface from time to time when Rachel's daughter, my mother, would recall something Rachel had done or said. My mother to this day is bothered by the closed-in forested climes of her later life—Arkansas, Virginia, Pennsylvania, Connecticut, and Georgia. When I ask her what is wrong with a forest, she

I am having a constant dialogue with this land, but I have not reached the point where I can leave my cameras at home.

I'm always feeling my way along, detecting new bugs, new flowers, lizards, grasses, as if no one else had ever seen them.

Before the coming of the white man, all this grass had no interruption save the great rolling rivers and the trees, mostly cottonwood, oak, walnut, hickory, elm, sycamore, and ash, that grew along the rivers' courses.

answers almost wistfully, "I can't see any way but straight up."

A university degree, a husband, two sons, fifteen years of marriage, and a move to Kansas finally brought the prairie back to me; but even then I had no inkling that I would want to spend the following ten years, and perhaps the rest of my life, looking at prairies, walking on them, and trying to record what I see. Both my parents had early awakened in me a "sense of wonder" concerning the natural world, as Rachel Carson defined it, so that living in the midst of this gigantic landform and with the help of knowledgeable and patient people, I was able to put two and two together and "see the landscape." Finding the prairies, discovering new things about them and on them is like having Christmas all year round.

I am having a constant dialogue with this land, but I have not reached the point where I can leave my cameras at home. The cameras are a necessary nuisance, a crutch, extensions of my eyes and arms. It's as if I must prove to myself first of all, and to the world secondly, that I have seen these marvelous things. If I see milkweed silk glowing between me and the afternoon sun, I have to take a picture of it. I must admire those outdoor sojourners who enjoy the natural world without having to tell everyone and his cousin about it. Everything about the prairie is an event for me, and I seem compelled to soliloquize about the wonder of it. I'm always feeling my way along, detecting new bugs, new flowers, lizards, grasses, as if no one else had ever seen them. I am an excited child

on an Easter egg hunt.

But what is a prairie? That is a very good question, one that I am still pondering. The word itself is a French word meaning "meadow." One thing that no one disputes is that it is, or was, a landscape covering 750,000,000 acres in the middle of our country—hardly a "meadow." Its prime features were grass, sky, and space. "The land is in the shape of a ball . . . wherever a man stands he is surrounded by the sky" wrote Coronado's diarist in 1541 when his expedition reached Kansas. Before the coming of the white man, all this grass had no interruption save the great rolling rivers and the trees, mostly cottonwood, oak, walnut, hickory, elm, sycamore, and ash, that grew along the rivers' courses. "Grass owned the prairie" wrote Methodist Bishop John Quayle of Baldwin City, Kansas, in 1905. Scientists believe that the prairie is close to being the most complex, and yet the most balanced, ecosystem on earth. At the Save The Tallgrass Prairie Conference at Elmdale, Kansas, in 1973, Professor A. W. Küchler of Kansas University stated that "a climax prairie is so finely attuned to its environment and is so perfectly integrated into the ecosystem as a whole that one can only marvel."

There are three kinds of prairie within this enormous piece of property. To the east, just out of the forests, is the tallgrass, or true, prairie. Westward, as the rainfall lessens, the midgrasses become dominant. Still farther west, where the land rises toward the great wall of the Rocky Mountains, are the high plains, the shortgrass prairie.

The Tallgrass Prairie

My prairie journeys have the most to do with the tallgrass prairie. Most of this prairie lies within a land division that scientists call the central lowlands. This huge region covers parts or all of the states of Ohio, Indiana, Illinois, Wisconsin, Minnesota, Iowa, Missouri, Texas, Oklahoma, Kansas, Nebraska, and North and South Dakota. The tallgrass prairie once covered 400,000 square miles, and it was a teeming factory of life. It formerly supported eighty species of mammals, three hundred species of birds, and thousands of kinds of insects and other animal life. J. E. Weaver describes the true, or tallgrass, prairie as having level areas, knolls, steep bluffs, rolling hilly land, valleys, and extensive alluvial flood plains. Much of the form of the land and even the rivers' courses were molded by a series of ancient earth-grinding glaciers reaching down in various patterns from the north and then receding, with the most recent glacier ending some ten thousand years ago. The waters from the melting glaciers were another grand-scale sculptor's tool, washing and shaping the land and leaving behind all kinds of sediment: boulders, rocks, sand, and soil. Spiny and shell-encased water creatures, millions upon millions of them, lived and died in these glacial waters and deposited their skeletons on the bottom of each successive sea. These skeletons fused and became the layers of limestone that are prevalent in some tallgrass prairie areas. Other regions were left full of potholes of all sizes that continue to hold water to this day.

The tallgrass prairie dazzles the eye with an unending array of blooming plants, and this spectacle, with some seventeen new species coming into bloom each week, lasts from March until October. The tallgrasses themselves, big bluestem, indiangrass, switchgrass, and cordgrass, to name the common ones, are the most powerful, the most expansive, the most majestic of all the prairie plants; they are the redwoods of the prairie.

Since the last great glacier, the tallgrass prairie has evolved into a perfect balance of wind and water, plant and animal. Prairie flora and fauna through the millennia learned to withstand disease, frost, high winds, drought, fire, and severe heat. The climate bounces like a ping pong ball with nothing to hinder the great air masses coming up from the Gulf of Mexico and down from Canada.

Because of relatively abundant rainfall, the tallgrass prairie became the most intricate of the three kinds of prairies. The tallgrass prairie dazzles the eye with an unending array of blooming plants, and this spectacle, with some seventeen new species coming into bloom each week, lasts from March until October. The tallgrasses themselves, big bluestem, indiangrass, switchgrass, and cordgrass, to name the common ones, are the most powerful, the most expansive, the most majestic of all the prairie plants; they are the redwoods of the prairie, and, like the redwoods, they are vanishing.

Man surely adapted to the grasslands from very early times. Some fourteen million years ago a pre-man being named Ramapithecus by paleontologists came out of the forests of Africa onto the tallgrasslands of that continent. In order to survive, he had to learn to stand upright to see over the tallgrasses to observe his enemies and to hunt. Some of these grasses were the wild ancestors of modern wheat, barley, rye, oats, rice, and other cereals. Through the ages, Ramapithecus learned to cooperate in the hunt with his fellow beings, he developed a language, his brain grew larger, and he became man. I like to think of the tallgrasses as being the mother of present-day man.

There are many allusions to the tallgrass prairie in the early journals, diaries, and literature of our country. The invading Europeans were astounded as they moved west from the deep eastern forests. From the journals of those inland astronauts Lewis and Clark, July 12, 1804, we read: "The low land of the Missouri [is] covered with undulating grass nearly five feet high, gradually rising to a second plane, where rich weeds and flowers are interspersed with copses of Osage plum; further back are seen small groves of trees; an abundance of grapes; the wild cherry of the Missouri; and the choke-cherry which was observed for the first time." If Lewis and Clark had arrived in this area only a month later, the grasses they saw would have been eight to ten feet high.

In 1825, George Champlin Sibley observed: "The Herbage of this Plain in general [is] rich and luxuriant consisting chiefly of strong and succulent Grass of many varieties. Some of which would doubtless prove valuable additions to the cultivated grasses of the United States. In the season of flowers a very large portion of this great plain presents one continual carpet of Soft verdure, enriched by flowers of every tint."

Washington Irving wrote in his *Tour on the Prairies*, "It is delightful, in thus bivouaking on the prairies, to lie awake and gaze at the stars; it is like watching them from the deck of a ship at sea, when at one view we have the whole scope of heaven."

My Prairies

My home in Kansas is just beyond Kansas City at Lake Quivira; thus I live near the western edge of the original tall-grass prairie. On these outskirts of the city, there are still found a few small patches of primeval prairie that by some inexplicable accident have not been bulldozed or plowed into oblivion. There is one such fossil prairie approximately thirty acres in size just a short walk from my house, and I make it a point to visit it daily, if at all possible, because time spent here becomes far more than a mere visit for me. This prairie is my textbook, my oasis from the batterings of a normal day.

There is a much larger, almost intact, tallgrass prairie region just two hours drive west known as the Flint Hills. As far as is known, the Flint Hills, extending into the Osage Hills of northern Oklahoma, comprise the very last unplowed, though heavily grazed, tallgrass prairie of any size in North America. This area in Kansas, lying just west of Topeka, is peanut shaped on the map and is about two hundred miles from top to bottom, and about fifty miles wide. When establishing the route of the Santa Fe Trail from Independence, Missouri, in 1825, George Champlin Sibley wrote: "We . . . entered upon an almost boundless Prairie, which being rough and hilly, obliged us to travel a very crooked path for several Miles. The Prairie is very high and is generally strewed over with small flakes of Limestone and Flint." These Flint Hills are a perfect example of a landscape formed by the succession of primeval seas mentioned earlier. It is the presence of

limestone and flint and the "rough and hilly terrain" which preserved the landscape of the Flint Hills, unlike the rest of the tallgrass prairie, from the homesteader's plow.

The Flint Hills are unique in several ways. One can fly low over them in a small plane and see that they resemble a huge velvet, bronze-colored, disheveled quilt (or green or white depending on the season). The hills rise from the surrounding human-scored landscape like fused backs of a herd of ancient bison. They also resemble waves on an ocean, a succession of oscillating curves, swelling and cresting as far as the eye can see. The hills are a

The waters from the melting glaciers were another grand-scale sculptor's tool, washing and shaping the land and leaving behind all kinds of sediment: boulders, rocks, sand, and soil.

The Flint Hills rise from the surrounding human-scored landscape like fused backs of a herd of ancient bison.

living museum saved for us by chance, a time tunnel to our past. The Flint Hills are one face of many faces of the original tallgrass prairie. They are rugged, harsh, remote, primitive. Because they are a small distance from my home, I have set out to learn about the tallgrass prairie from them. The hills have become my bond with the earth, my proving ground. The hills put me in my place in the universe.

In the course of a year I make many trips to the Flint Hills. Often my destination is the Konza Prairie. The Konza is some 8,600 acres of fenced-off, preserved tallgrass prairie which was previously a working cattle ranch, and is now leased to Kansas State University by the Nature Conservancy, a national, privately funded, non-profit organization. The conservancy's sole objective is to purchase diverse samples of natural landscape in the United States for preservation. The Konza Prairie is named for the earliest-known people to occupy the area—the Konza, Kansas, or Kaw Indians, the People of the South Wind. The Konza is the largest protected tallgrass prairie in the

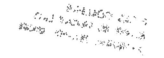

United States, and its topography is typical of the rest of the Flint Hills with the added feature of hundreds of kinds of untrammelled tallgrasses and other plants. This prairie is presently being managed by the biology department of Kansas State University to approximate the presettlement tallgrass prairie ecosystem with the exception of the presence of the large grazing mammals. It is being used for long-term research projects by students and faculty of the university. It is not open to the public.

Because the tallgrass prairie was perfectly "managed" for countless centuries without help from the white man through an intricate interdependence of natural forces including fire, wind, and millions of grazing, nomadic, hoofed herbivores, the Konza with its absence of these wild grasseaters must be managed by a series of man-made techniques. The principal technique used here is controlled burning. Man-made management on other, much smaller, prairies elsewhere includes mowing and light grazing by cattle. Both natural forces and man-made techniques are essential to keep a prairie a prairie. If the seeds of trees and woody plants from other areas, unceasingly borne to all corners of all prairies by birds and wind, are allowed to gain a toehold, the area becomes a scrub forest within a generation. Fire kills seedling trees but does not kill the deep-rooted grasses which sometimes reach twelve feet into the ground. Because of good management—as close to natural conditions as is possible—walking the Konza's trails is a lesson from the pages of history, not to mention a profound aesthetic experience.

The Konza Prairie is very close to a description of the original tallgrass prairie as written by Edwin Bryant, a California emigrant, in 1846:

As we approached what is called the . . . prairie, the road became much drier and less difficult. The vast prairie itself soon opened before us in all its grandeur and beauty. I had never before beheld extensive scenery of this kind. The many descriptions of the prairies of the west had forestalled in some measure the first impressions produced by the magnificent landscape spread out before me as far as the eye could reach, bounded alone by the blue wall of the sky. No description, however, which I have read of these scenes, or which can be written, can convey more than a faint impression to the imagination of their effects upon the eye. The view of the illimitable succession of green undulations and flowery slopes, of every gentle and graceful configuration, stretching away and away, until they fade from the sight in the dim distance, creates a wild and scarcely controllable ecstacy of admiration. I felt, I doubt not, some of the emotions natural to the aboriginal inhabitants of these boundless and picturesque plains, when roving with unrestrained freedom over them; and careless alike of the past and the future, luxuriating in the blooming wilderness of sweets which the Great Spirit had created for their enjoyment, and placed at their disposal.

The remaining tallgrass prairie other than the Flint Hills has been reduced to tiny islands dotted over the aforementioned states. In recent years, I have been ranging not only over the Flint Hills, but also have dauntlessly ventured from prairie island to prairie island, taking pictures and talking to people connected with the land. I am collecting tallgrass prairies and the life

Often my destination is the Konza Prairie. The Konza is some 8,600 acres of fenced-off, preserved tallgrass prairie which was previously a working cattle ranch.

On these outskirts of the city, there are still found a few small patches of primeval prairie that by some inexplicable accident have not been bulldozed into oblivion.

upon them. There is work here for several lifetimes.

The prairie is a state of mind as much as it is a place, this heaving, wild, outlandishly beautiful landscape, coming down to us from millions of earth-seasons. One does not just go out and "do" the prairie and go on to something else. A single look-see will give you nothing. That is why millions of Americans drive straight through Kansas and other prairie states without stopping.

The wild tallgrass prairie must be allowed to seep into all of America's consciousness. From it we can reread our history and our character. Isn't there some correlation between a free, open landscape and a free, open people? From undisturbed prairie, scientists have a measuring stick to study healthy soil and such things as new sources of drought resistant grain foods.

There must be many trips, many seasons for us to learn about the land of our forefathers. Indeed the most enduring, endearing, demanding dimension of the prairies is the change from season to season. Rachel Carson wrote: "Those who dwell, as scientists or laymen, among the beauties and mysteries of the earth are never alone or weary of life. There is something infinitely healing in the repeated refrains of nature—the assurance that dawn comes after night and spring after winter."

YEAR OF THE PRAIRIE
WINTER

The prairie is closed down, out to lunch as they say, in winter. November habitually provides a thick-layered, gray cloud-screen of a sky and the first hard freeze, ringing down the curtain on the dazzling colors of October. The goldenrod turns brownish gray; the sumac turns black; insects burrow or die; and the grasses turn all shades of tan to deep brown bronze. As John C. Van Tramp wrote in his *Prairie and Rocky Mountain Adventures* in 1866, "I have seen the prairies when the first winter's frost fell upon them, their green verdure changed to a light yellow, almost white; the tall dry grass lying flat and motionless."

Iowa Prairies

There is a steady, hard rain as my husband Herb and I drive north in early November for a rendezvous with some of the preserved prairies in Iowa, the one state that was mostly covered with tallgrass. The land here has already turned into its November colors. We arrive after dark at the Ames Holiday Inn for a meeting with Dean Roosa, Iowa State Preserves Board Ecologist, and he briefs us about the next day's tour. The prairie preservation and restoration movement began in Iowa in 1933 with the Iowa Academy of Science which prepared "The Iowa Twenty-Five Year Conservation Plan" for the state conservation commission. This plan, among other things, proposed the concept of preserves and named seventy areas in need of preservation. Dr. Ada Hayden, professor of botany at Iowa State University, outlined a more detailed plan in her report, "The Selection of Prairie Areas in Iowa which Should Be Preserved." As a result of Dr. Hayden's work, the first four tracts of tallgrass prairie were purchased by the state. The largest of these, 240 acres, was owned by one family for seventy-eight years when it was purchased in 1945 and was named after Dr. Hayden. The Hayden Prairie, still the largest state-owned tract, is four miles west of Lime Springs in northeast Iowa.

The Iowa State Preserve System was

November habitually provides a thick-layered, gray cloud-screen of a sky and the first hard freeze, ringing down the curtain on the dazzling colors of October.

JOSEPH B. CLAY PRAIRIE
THE PRESERVATION OF THIS NATIVE
IOWA PRAIRIE WAS MADE POSSIBLE
THROUGH GIFTS TO THE STATE COLLEGE
OF IOWA FOUNDATION.
IT IS NAMED FOR MR. JOSEPH B. CLAY,
A GRADUATE AND LONG TIME FRIEND
OF THE COLLEGE, WHO WAS THE PRIME
MOVER IN PRESERVING THIS BIT OF
OUR IOWA HERITAGE.

The Iowa State Preserve System was created by the Iowa legislature in 1965, and since then thirty-two areas have been dedicated.

"I have pictures of the prairie. You would say, 'That isn't a picture of anything—just space.' That was our environment—space. We learned to love it just as the Swiss love the Alps. This open prairie."

"The grasshoppers just cleaned up. There was nothing left."

created by the Iowa legislature in 1965, and since then thirty-two areas have been dedicated. As stated in the Directory of State Preserves: "The nature preserves serve as living museums and are to be used in a manner consistent with their continued preservation for educational use, scientific research, and for use by the many generations which follow us. These preserves also serve as genetic reservoirs and sanctuaries for our vanishing native plant and animal communities and often provide habitat for species which have become so scarce that we now call them 'threatened' or 'endangered'." I just can't help stating here that I admire the Iowa legislature for its degree of awareness of the need for prairie preservation. This awareness is as advanced as that of the state of Kansas is behind, but there is some evidence that Kansas is catching up.

After coffee and a late evening snack, we agree to meet Dean again before daylight the next morning for a tour of one day to as many state prairies as possible. The coffee shop breakfast is as dismal as the weather outside—it still rains cats and dogs. We start out remembering with hope that it could clear into that fresh, translucent, after-rain light that is well known on the prairie.

The rain has slowed to a drizzle as we drive toward Clay Prairie in Butler County. The Iowa landscape is clear and flat and brown. The tiny 2.64-acre Clay Prairie was purchased in 1961 by the University of Northern Iowa and named for Joseph B. Clay, the person responsible for its preservation. In spite of its minute size, it supports at least ninety-eight species of plants. In May hundreds of shooting stars can be

seen, and this is soon followed by purple avens, indian paintbrush, downy gentian, and rattlesnake master. The Clay Prairie was dedicated as a state preserve in 1976.

We drive to another unnamed twenty-acre prairie, which like Clay Prairie is beside an old cemetery. At the moment, the state is looking into the feasibility of adding this tract to its preserve system. By this time, the purple gray sky is churning out another heavy downpour, and we decide to drive to the next town for lunch, still hoping for a productive day. Alas, there is no hope; it rains harder than ever after lunch. Dean drives us back to Ames, we pick up our car and turn south to home without beginning to see the fine network of Iowa state prairies. There is a vow to Dean to return in the spring.

Child of the Frontier

During November there is another trip, this time to accompany Herb to San Diego where he is to speak to a group of architects. I want to go because I have learned that a ninety-nine-year-old survivor of frontier Kansas, Alma Ise Lindley, lives there now in the care of her children. I have longed for a firsthand account of wilderness prairie, and this is my chance. The Ise family is well known in the annals of Kansas. The late Professor John Ise of Kansas University, Alma's younger brother, was a prolific writer. A scholar, historian, and an active lover of national parks, he wrote "Our National Park Policy, A Critical History" in 1961. He also wrote "Sod and Stubble," a vivid account of the Ise family's settlement in 1870s Kansas.

I find Alma in the older section of San Diego in one of those marvelous 1920s Japanese/California bungalows. She is in a wheelchair due to a recent fall. Her body and voice are worn out, but her mind is quick and strong. As we talk, her eyes reach back to the wild prairie of her youth in Kansas:

My parents were married in 1873. The first baby, little Albert, lived only five months. My mother had a pretty hard time. Her breasts caked, and the baby was not very strong. It was a very hot summer, and the cows' milk would sour even when they hung it in the well.

I remember how the prairie looked in the 1870s. My mother's sister stayed with us—and she used to haul me all over the prairies in a little wagon.

My father's account of the coming of the grasshoppers to Kansas was very vivid. The grasshoppers just cleaned up. There was nothing left. The people lived on corn meal during the winter. There was no fruit, no train to bring anything in. My mother used to laugh because she thought I was born hungry for fruit. I used to wonder how a woman who was so poorly nourished could give birth to such a vigorous child that would grow to live almost one hundred years. I guess science has proved that nature will take care of the fetus first and the mother second. That is the usual thing. At any rate, I put it to the test.

We saw Indians all the time. We would see two or three Indians with a horse and kind of "drag." There would be a baby or two on it, or maybe an old warrior. They would go past the house. My most vivid recollection of the Indians—my mother and father had gone to shop in town, Cawker City, so she left "Old Frank" in charge. He was awfully soft for the Indians. Of course, the Indians had had a bad deal. We'll

The first snows on the tallgrass prairie cover even the muted November after-freeze colors and wipe the slate clean.

"I have seen the prairies when the first winter's frost fell upon them, their green verdure changed to a light yellow, almost white; the tall dry grass lying flat and motionless."

admit that. Whenever he saw an Indian, "Old Frank" wanted to make amends in all kinds of ways. A couple of Indians came along and wanted to come in. Of course, it was only a one-room house. There was no place for us children to go so we crawled under the bed. And we had to cry because we were scared. The grownups would tell terrible stories of atrocities, so we were plenty scared of Indians. The Indians told Frank they were hungry. "Old Frank" sliced up all the bacon my mother had and cooked it for the Indians. Used all the eggs she had been saving too. She only had a dozen hens who didn't have many eggs. I believe he made some biscuits and used all the lard she had. Apparently, the Indians appreciated the meal and ate everything. These were either Kiowas or Comanches. After they left, we came out from under the bed. My brother cried so hard he vomited. I cried too. When my mother came home, she gave Frank a real good scolding for frightening us children so much. He knew we were afraid of anything Indian—turkey feathers and such.

About the time of the Kansas-Nebraska Act, people would break a little patch of prairie and plant corn or vegetables, and it would be miles before you'd see another broken plot. People would borrow food from each other when they ran out.

On a good spring day the wagons were moving west. Then no rain, no rain, no rain. The heat and the drought—they had nothing to eat—we couldn't do much for the people who stopped by. We shared things as best we could.

The early home was a log cabin. We didn't have a sod house—that was more primitive. I don't know where my father got the logs. He had come down in the fall of '71 after he had made a downpayment on a farm in Iowa. He had made some money breaking the prairie for a pretty good salary. He bought a wagon and a

breaking plow. For that he had to have a harness and such. There was a stipulated price for breaking sod because all that whole Midwest had to be broken. It was all in sod in the beginning. My father got $1.25 an acre for breaking prairie. He had saved about $300 for his farm. He wrapped his money up and stuck it in his pocket. When he got home from the bank, the money was not there. He looked and looked but never found it. The Homestead Act had just been passed so he planned to start over in Kansas.

I have pictures of the prairie. You would say, "That isn't a picture of anything—just space." That was our environment—space. We learned to love it just as the Swiss love the Alps. This open prairie. The wildflowers were beautiful. I used to pick the wildflowers. The ones we had—we called them daisies. They were anemones that grew on the prairie. I remember I wore a little apron, and I'd put my flowers in there, and I'd see that one was misfit. I'd feel sorry for it and pick it so it wouldn't be left in the wilderness. I thought the flowers liked me as well as I liked them—so I'd want to pick them and take them home.

Alma passed away a few months after my visit, just before her one hundredth birthday. I shall never forget this remarkable lady who spoke in poetry.

Winter Curtain

The first snows on the tallgrass prairie cover even the muted November after-freeze colors and wipe the slate clean. They blow down in a fury out of a storm born in Canada, come on down the Dakotas, and hit the Flint Hills near the time of Thanksgiving. During a snowstorm, the horizon, so much a part of the prairie in other seasons, is blotted out, so that earth and sky, instead of constantly sparring with each trying to outdo the other in brilliance and color, become one. Land and sky are indistinguishable until the storm passes, and once again the shining, clear-blue dome reigns now over a crystal, cold-white world.

In winter, as in every other season, I make almost daily trips to "my" prairie at Lake Quivira. On the coldest days, I will trudge through the deep path worn by motorcyclists, and I barely get a dozen steps along before I must stop for a picture of the light coming through the ice-covered stems of big bluestem, or some other equally meritorious object.

Good boots are a must in winter as they are throughout the year. On the Konza the snow-covered, pockmarked limestone and flint rocks can break an ankle; the bronze grasses are still upright, a rigid mass; and one must pick out a direction very carefully. It seems that after a snow, the winds become quiet for a time, and if you trample the grass or snap a twig with its ice covering, the sounds reverberate and bounce all over the hills. Sometimes in the morning sun an entire cascade of ice will fall from the limbs of a cottonwood and will sound like a Japanese glass windchime. Winter on the prairie seems forbidding, but even at such a time I think of Thoreau's words, "Each season seems best to us in its turn."

On the coldest days, I will trudge through the deep path worn by motorcyclists, and I barely get a dozen steps along before I must stop for a picture of the light coming through the ice-covered big bluestem.

YEAR OF THE PRAIRIE
SPRING

We start looking for spring late in February, but that is always too early. Winter does not let go without a wrestle, and everyone gets anxious. I walk on my Quivira prairie looking down low into the grass for any sign of life. I also drive and drive in the Flint Hills to find spring, knowing it will happen some afternoon when I'm not looking. The red-tailed hawks are out scrutinizing the landscape for good eating. Any perch will do. Their pure white breasts flash in the sun when I am driving to the hills. They populate this busiest of Kansas traffic corridors, the turnpike, in fair numbers staring haughtily at all cars. I have seen them swoop just in front of oncoming cars, catching a quarry, perhaps a field mouse that somehow made it to the median strip. Or I have seen them soaring between me and the sun, red tail flashing, a translucent fan. Hawks taunt photographers. If you stop your car to take a picture, they are off in a split second to perch again just out of camera range.

I am looking for any kind of life on the warmer spring days. I have great expectations at the end of February and all during March. I think I see a pink flower embedded deep within the dead winter grasses at the Quivira prairie. My first flower! I lean over for a closer look. Could this be a rare early bloomer? Anything can happen in spring, and I am ready. It is plastic! It is a dime-store flower like the ones you see on Memorial Day wreaths. I walk on, disconcerted, but eventually I am satisfied with the wisps of grass just showing out of the ground with dew still on it. Meadowlarks are sounding some distance away. Life returns. Life endures.

Birds are beginning their long flights north. Wild geese, the snows and Canadas, are honking and flying over my house. I am like jelly, shameless and silly, when I hear migrating geese. I dance about and yell to the dogs, "Do you see them? Do you hear them?" My birdfeeders at home are thick with warblers, chickadees, goldfinches, titmouses, and the old standbies—cardinals and bluejays. I hear other timid ones sing-

The redbuds are the first color. Their blossoms shine out on the highway like pink banners in a parade.

I drive and drive in the Flint Hills to find spring, knowing it will happen some afternoon when I'm not looking.

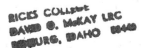

It is easy to picture these birds as the next thing to flying reptiles.... Fossils of sandhill cranes found in Nebraska indicate their presence on the Platte River area 10 million years ago.

ing their heads off: the thrashers, the yellow-billed cuckoo, the mockingbird, but I don't see them. Their songs are lovely.

The Flint Hills are still brown; not enough green is showing to make a difference in March and early April. The redbuds are the first color. Their blossoms shine out on the highway like pink banners in a parade. There must be many persons beside myself who gauge spring by the appearance of the redbuds.

Sandhill Cranes

This is the spring that I have vowed to see the sandhill cranes at their stopping place on the Platte River in central Nebraska. On Good Friday morning my husband Herb and I and two other couples pack our gear into the Blazer and head north. Each spring about seventy percent of the world's lesser sandhill cranes, about 200,000 of them, crowd into a 150-mile stretch of the Platte River near Kearney, Nebraska. This is the neck of an hourglass-shaped migration route. The cranes gather here like clockwork every spring from wintering grounds in Texas, New Mexico, California, Arizona, and northern and central Mexico. They stop here to rest, to preen feathers, to dance, to mate (cranes mate for life), and to gather strength for the next long leg of their migration. Their destinations are various locations in central Canada, Alaska, and Siberia.

Several subspecies of sandhill cranes still exist in North America: the non-migratory Florida and the Cuban sandhill cranes which number only 600 and 100 respectively; the greater, intermediate and lesser

sandhill cranes, which are all migratory and all pass through Nebraska. The greater sandhills number about 10,000, and the intermediate population is not known. As for the lesser sandhill cranes, which still exist in impressive numbers, their name seems a misnomer. They are commanding, archaic-looking birds standing almost four feet tall, weighing six to eight pounds, and have a wingspread of six feet. They have long, blue black legs, topped with an ash gray body, a long neck extending into a neon-red crested head, red eyes, and a long, sharp beak. It is easy to picture these birds as the next thing to flying reptiles, and, indeed, their remains have been found in sediment from the Eocene period of 55 million years ago. Fossils of sandhill cranes found in Nebraska indicate their presence on the Platte River area 10 million years ago.

Our campground destination for seeing the cranes is the Fort Kearney Recreation Area near historic Fort Kearney, an important outpost in the 1850s on the Oregon Trail. The drive to Fort Kearney from Kansas City takes six or seven hours. As we drive west in Nebraska from Grand Island, we begin to see small clusters of cranes flying toward the river. They look like flying crosses; they do not tuck their long necks back in flight as the great blue herons do; necks and legs are both extended straight out, and the flight is a graceful glide in a V-formation. Now we can also hear them. They make a sort of echoing chortle, quite unlike the honk of geese or any other bird we have heard. There is plenty of light left to set up camp when we arrive at the campsite. After a delicious chicken dinner cooked over charcoal, we settle in for a good night of sleep.

In crane country you rise early. Cranes roost in the shallow Platte River at night but begin moving out to the fields early to feed on left-over grain, insects, and grub worms. We had arranged a meeting at the National Audubon Society's Sanctuary at Gibbon with Bob Wicht, the manager, at 6.00 A.M. The light on the river is perfect, and we spend the morning observing and photographing the cranes from the Audubon tower, a rather comfortable, enclosed structure. On this particular morning, there are just a fair number of birds visible from our vantage point, not the great numbers I have read about. Bob informs us that we are a little late, that 95 percent of the birds have already flown north. After the birds leave the river, we spend the remainder of the day eating breakfast, resting, touring Fort Kearney, and walking along the Platte hoping to see other wildlife.

At 6:00 P.M. we again drive the short distance to the observation tower to watch the cranes coming in for the night. There are still many, many cranes in spite of our unfortunate timing. As we reach the tower, Bob invites me to join him farther on down the river, and as we drive in his four-wheel drive, I sense that he is excited about something. Suddenly we stop, and I follow him on foot through masses of bushes and grass to a viewing spot facing the setting sun. The river is vibrating with color, pink and orange, and it is criss-crossed with reflections of the still bare trees. We hear

flutters and cackles as a large flock of white pelicans lands on a sand bar just in front of us. Bob advises me to look at them carefully through my long lens as he casually mentions that word is out that whooping cranes have been sighted coming in this direction. I strain for my first glimpse ever of a whooping crane, but, alas, there are none. I am almost as pleased to see the pelicans and watch their ungainly efforts to catch fish and fit them into their pouches. In a positive step, the U. S. Fish and Wildlife Service recently designated this area criti-

Cranes roost in the shallow Platte River at night but begin moving out to the fields early to feed on left-over grain, insects, and grub worms.

cal to the survival of the whooping crane.

As we drive back to the tower after the light is gone, Bob gives me more information about cranes and their tenuous hold on life. Although they seem plentiful, this piece of the Platte River is one of the last roosting grounds meeting their exacting requirements, and this area is threatened with man's ever present callousness toward his fellow earthly creatures. In spite of the recent protective designation, the powerful forces that profit from dams are still at work to ruin the Platte for cranes. The big birds are also threatened this year with the dreaded fowl cholera disease.

Our second night at the campground is punctuated with a wild south wind that never lets us sleep. We rise early to the call of an angry male western meadowlark. It seems that we have invaded his territory, but his call is music to me, and I am glad he is singing so close to us. As the crane chortles come overhead and bobwhite quail are calling in the background, I note to myself that this is some kind of church for Easter Sunday! After a morning walk to the river, we cook and eat breakfast and then pack up the tents to begin the long drive home.

The Konza Burn

April is busy. On the third Saturday of the month Herb and I have been invited to the Konza Prairie by Dr. Lloyd Hulbert of Kansas State University to witness the annual spring burn. The Konza is divided into two sections, the "new" and the "old." The "new" section, some 7,700 acres bordering the "old" on the north and west, comprises

the historic Dewey Ranch and was purchased at the end of 1976. The old Konza, 916 acres, has been in existence since 1971 and has been managed by fire at various intervals at various locations for research purposes since then. There are areas that are burned at one-, two-, four- and ten-year intervals, with one area receiving no burning. As Dr. Hulbert puts it, "It will take many years to properly assess the different fire treatments." Before the burn, the entire "old" Konza has been embroidered with wide firebreaks, a technique of mowing and burning the dead winter grass down to the ground in ten- to twelve-foot corridors. These corridors divide the areas to be burned from those not to be burned and help control the fire.

As we arrive, we can see that just the tiniest sprigs of big bluestem and the other grasses are emerging from the firebreaks, forming an irregular pattern of green ribbons across the land. To the right and to the left of the firebreaks, the rich residue of tall bronze winter grasses is still intact. The early spring wildflowers that are seen favor the firebreaks because they do not have to push so hard to reach the sun; nevertheless, they do find a way to bloom everywhere. There are ground plum, blue-eyed grass, and wild indigo.

Upon walking into the Konza, we can see that the first burns are already occurring. Students with torches fueled with gasoline and diesel are seen on distant ridges setting more fires. As we walk through a burned area, the soot is dislodged with every step. It saturates hair, clothes, nostrils, and cameras. The odor of the burned grass is pun-

We rise early to the call of an angry male western meadowlark. It seems that we have invaded his territory.

The river is vibrating with color, pink and orange, and it is crisscrossed with reflections of the still bare trees. We hear flutters and cackles as a large flock of white pelicans lands on a sand bar just in front of us.

gent, but the smoke from areas that are still burning is downright forbidding. The flames that consume the dry grasses are ten to twenty feet high; they are awesome and terrible. One is forced to imagine the horrors of the wild prairie fires that consumed many lives and much property in the early days of white settlement. An old settler in Wabaunsee County, Kansas, recently recalled in the *Kansas City Star* fighting prairie fires: "Sometimes we had some thrilling experiences fighting fire. The wind would change with a rush in the night, and you would awake with the whole country ablaze, making lively work to save stock and stables, and we did not always save them."

The flames crackle and lick up and around the Konza hills at a slow uniform pace, sparing nothing. The sound and speed of the fire intensifies as the wind catches it, and it drowns out all other sounds even the alarmed and frightened meadowlarks. George Catlin wrote as an artist of the beauty of natural prairie fires: "The prairies burning form some of the most beautiful scenes that are to be witnessed in the country, and also some of the most sublime. Every acre of these vast prairies (being covered for hundreds and hundreds of miles with a crop of grass, which dies and dries in fall) burns over during the fall or early spring, leaving the ground of black and doleful color."

In other areas of the Flint Hills, the spring sky is filled with the smoke of many burnings. It is considered good rangeland practice, and, indeed, it is often written into the contracts of leased grazing land

As we arrive, we can see that just the tiniest sprigs of big bluestem and the other grasses are emerging from the firebreaks, forming an irregular pattern of green ribbons across the land.

"The prairies burning form some of the most beautiful scenes that are to be witnessed in the country, and also some of the most sublime. Every acre of these vast prairies (being covered for hundreds and hundreds of miles with a crop of grass, which dies and dries in fall) burns over during the fall or early spring, leaving the ground of black and doleful color."

Students with torches fueled with gasoline and diesel are seen on distant ridges setting more fires.

The color of the fire becomes progressively more intense as daylight diminishes. Fantastic orange dancing spikes form a massive ring on a far ridge.

On one side of the trail all the land's black with just a hint of green beginning to show. On the other side is an unburned still winter-looking prairie.

On any given booming ground, there are several dominant males, each defending a territory.

As the faintest morning light appears, there is a flutter of wings right outside the tent, and I can barely see that thirty or forty chickens have appeared like magic.

that the land must be burned every year. It is well known that burning will maximize expected weight gain for the lessee's cattle. Prairie rangeland researchers and many ranchers, however, believe that yearly burning is too often for the good health of the grass.

We make our way around the fire to a miniscule man-made pond that was built in the days when the Konza was still a cattle ranch. There on the bank on bare ground is a small snake, seemingly frozen with fear of the fire. It is an age-old fear from centuries of prairie fires that served to teach prairie creatures to endure the worst of calamities and be the stronger for it.

The heavy smoke from a farther fire is rising now between me and the setting sun. The *color* of the fire becomes progressively more intense as daylight diminishes. Fantastic orange dancing spikes form a massive ring on a far ridge. The landscape is a blazing inferno.

Camping with the Prairie Chickens

Just one week after the burning, I am on the Konza again for my first solo camping experience. This time I will be on the old Dewey Ranch, the "new" Konza, and I will pitch my tent in the middle of a "booming" ground of a flock of prairie chickens. "Booming" is the name of the spring ritual of the male greater prairie chicken as he vies for the attention of the female.

I am met at the Konza gate by John Zimmerman, a professor of ornithology at Kansas State University. John offers the Konza ATV (all terrain vehicle) to me as

backpacking all my gear to the booming ground would be difficult. I gratefully accept with some trepidation this strange jeep-tractor hybrid, but on a trial run I seem to master it rather quickly. John helps me transfer the gear from car to hybrid and gives me directions to the booming ground. It is three or four miles in a northwesterly direction beyond the border of the "old" Konza. I am to follow a firebreak to an open gate bordering the two Konza sections and then follow a cow path to a buffalo wallow where I am to see an old army tent that students have been using. The booming ground, I am told, is on a very high ridge facing north with a spectacular view. "You can't miss it," says John. I fervently hope that these are not famous last words. When one is alone on these hills, one is alone; there is a notable absence of landmarks, certainly an absence of people, and all the hills tend to look just alike.

John tells me more about the chickens before I take my leave. They are so colorful, so interesting and were once so numerous that many Indian dances and costumes were modeled after them. The chickens once ranged by the millions over the entire central lowlands area and much of the Great Plains. I recall reading George Catlin's description as he stayed at Fort Leavenworth in the 1820s: "This delicious bird is generally called the prairie hen and from what I can learn is much like the English grouse in size, color and habits. They appear in the months of August and September from the higher latitudes, where they go in the early part of the summer to raise their broods. This is the season for

I have become so beguiled by the prairie chickens, I decide I must learn, firsthand, more about them.

Buford Welch has real affection for his birds. For the favored pairs of prairie chickens, there are special name plates on the doors of the pens.

them, and the whole garrison, in fact, are almost subsisting on them at this time." I can only reflect that it was very stupid of the white man to almost wipe out such a marvelous bird, not to mention a readily available source of food for future generations.

There are three kinds of prairie chickens in the United States: the greater prairie chicken (the one I am stalking and the most numerous); the lesser prairie chicken, far fewer in number, whose habitat coincides with the greater in some areas; and the Attwater's prairie chicken, all living in southeast Texas and numbering only 2,000 birds. There was a fourth, the heath hen, now extinct, whose habitat was the coastal prairies along the north Atlantic seaboard.

The greater prairie chicken is a member of the grouse family and is about the size of a regular barnyard chicken. "Booming"—the rather exotic and dramatic, almost comical, ritual dance and sound of the male as he struts about to attract the hen—begins late in February on the designated grounds and lasts well into May. Usually the hens do not come to the grounds in significant numbers until late in the season. This is just as well because early nests would probably be destroyed by range fires.

As I drive the ATV toward my destination, I get an overall view of last week's burning; on one side of the trail all the land is black with just a hint of green beginning to show. On the other side is an unburned, still winter-looking prairie. As I cross over into the Dewey Ranch area of the Konza,

the difference in ungrazed and recently grazed land is remarkable. The grazed land looks scrubby and contains many plants other than grass. Fortunately, this section will recover in a few years. Soon I do find the tent and the buffalo wallow, and I know that I have arrived. The sun is very low over the hills by now so I hurry to set up my tent and settle in for the night. I explore the territory and take a few sunset pictures.

Before dawn I am awakened by human, not chicken, sounds. Frightened at first, I realize that these are students coming to use the army tent to observe the birds. As the faintest morning light appears, there is a flutter of wings right outside the tent, and I can barely see that thirty or forty chickens have appeared like magic. The show is beginning, and I have a ringside seat. On any given booming ground, there are several dominant males, each defending a territory, and many young males who don't seem to know what to do. If one male invades another's territory, there is a face-off, and feathers fly as the two jump up in a mock, posturing sort of duel. Other males, as the sun gives more light to the scene, proceed with the ritual dance and boom, a series of high-speed circular, or forward, dance steps, the head lowered, head feathers up, the tail fanning out, and the strangest thing of all—huge, orange purple bordered airsacs on the neck appear and flash like fluorescent globes as a three-toned "oo-a-oo" sound is emitted. This sequence is fervently repeated over and over again. It is a three-ring circus.

Into all this activity calmly struts the female. This feverish display is solely for her benefit, and yet she makes a great effort to appear totally engrossed in pecking at the grass. After an hour or so of this activity, the dominant male mounts her, and mating is fulfilled. Presumably, the hen then goes to a remote spot to make her grass-covered nest and lay her dozen or so eggs. Promptly at nine o'clock on this particular morning all the chickens fly away except one or two stragglers. As I must get some circulation back into my feet, I stand up outside my tent, and these last fellows fly away also.

I am exhausted and hungry so I hike to the gate (not wanting to drive the ATV again until I have to), drive into Manhattan for breakfast, come back to my campsite for a long rest, more exploration and picture taking, and then I settle in to await the evening "boom." This boom is less passionate, but I do get some good shots, I think, into the setting sun. (My tent door faces west.) The next morning the entire three-ring spectacle is repeated, and I devour rolls and rolls of film. My God, this show cannot have many equals. Again the birds all leave promptly at nine o'clock. It's almost like the world of business. I begin to secure the camp wearily, load the ATV, and drive back to the Konza entrance about noon. After another good "storebought" breakfast, I'm going back to my home with a full bounty of prairie chicken pictures. Good hunting!

The Prairie Chicken Man

I have become so beguiled by the prairie chickens, I decide I must learn, firsthand, more about them. My good friend, Profes-

34

Buford Welch is a jovial, unpretentious man who has observed prairie chickens in the wild for as long as he can remember. Four years ago, alarmed at the fast decline of the bird in eastern Kansas, he decided to try to breed them in captivity.

sor E. Raymond Hall of Kansas University, had told me some time ago about a man in southeast Kansas who raises prairie chickens successfully in captivity, one of the very few able to do so. His name is Buford Welch, and he owns a bait shop in Moran, Kansas. I make an appointment with him by telephone and settle on a day in the middle of the last week in April. Mr. Welch assures me that he has several males still booming and several hens on nests.

The drive south to Moran in late April is especially pleasant. Once the gently rolling country was all tallgrass prairie, and now the land is almost entirely cultivated. The farms look prosperous and clean. Occasionally, one can still see patches of virgin prairie from the highway, and of course in late April these prairies are beginning to bloom.

Moran is a typical one-main-street, nineteenth-century-looking Kansas community. A banner stretched across the main street proudly proclaims "Home Town of Miss America, Debbie Barnes." This event occurred several years ago, but it is still cause for community pride. Welch's Bait Shop is at the first intersection of the main street, and his prairie chickens reside behind the shop in specially constructed chicken-wire pens along with separate pens for quail and for chukkar, a game bird from India.

Buford Welch is a jovial, unpretentious man who has observed prairie chickens in the wild for as long as he can remember. Four years ago, alarmed at the fast decline of the bird in eastern Kansas, he decided to try to breed them in captivity. Although

Welch, in addition to his bait business, holds a position as field superintendent of the oil field section of the Kansas State Corporation Commission, he has had no formal academic study in any of the area colleges or universities. There is just a simple declaration, "I always figured I could raise them." Now several university professors, including well-known prairie exponents such as my friend Raymond Hall, are interested in his methods. Welch is a member of the American Game Bird Breeders' Federation and won the Outstanding Game Bird Breeders' Propagation Award in 1972.

In the beginning there were problems with the chickens. The first male birds raised to adulthood from incubated eggs found in the wild would not boom. Now Welch realizes the pens he built were too small, and the ground in the pens was covered with gravel—a surface which was too rough for the males. The gravel made their feet sore and so they would not dance. And also there was not enough room for the male to lay out a territory for his full mating display. The new pens now measure twelve feet by thirty feet, and they are five feet high. Welch also learned the hard way not to put two males in the same pen. Penned up cocks will fight to the death, unlike those in the wild, and he lost one for this reason.

As he conquered the problems of booming and mating, Welch's man-made shelters of hay and grasses did seem to aid the hens in making nests and laying their eggs. He finds that the hens lay about the same number of eggs as in the wild, ranging in number from twelve to twenty. Prairie chickens, like other wild game birds, lay their eggs in the afternoon, usually one each day. The mother hen places grass or straw over each egg as it appears until all are laid. Then begins the setting period which lasts about three weeks. The male does not assist the hen in any way either before or after the eggs hatch. From experience with his other game birds, Welch believes that the prairie chicken is the only species that will stay on a nest and hatch its young in captivity.

There were difficulties in feeding the young chicks. Welch found that at first, after hatching healthy chicks, many of them developed a paralysis or a deformity of the legs and toes. Welch now believes that the cause was a diet deficiency. His method of feeding the chicks always has been meticulous and time consuming. He has constructed special brooding boxes with light bulbs at one end for constant heat, and he finds it necessary to take the chicks from the mother within twenty-four hours after hatching for careful feeding and observation for the first four weeks. "For the very first food I advocate a kind of custard or cottage cheese and small meal worms," he tells me. "In the natural state the mother softens the food in her mouth before giving it to her offspring." Welch also tells me he adds "succulent greens" to the above menu.

After two weeks he adds chips of game bird pellets softened with warm water. As a separate side dish, the chicks are given cooked egg yolks put through a fine sieve. All of this is fed in fresh portions three times a day. Gradually, the soft food is changed to dry pellets, but he continues the greens as the major portion. As the chicks grow older, Welch adds cut grasses, dandelions, clover, and alfalfa. Occasionally, there are fruits for the chicks: berries, grapes, and apples.

Welch feels that part of the cause of the decline of the wild bird, besides the plowing up and paving over of the native grasses, is the eating of grasses from chemicalized or poisoned soil. As for the foot deformity problem, even after the seemingly balanced feeding program, some of the chicks were affected. For the solution, Welch contacted Dr. C. R. Creger of the Poultry Science Department of Texas A. & M. University. Dr. Creger has been successful in raising the Attwater's prairie chicken in captivity but had experienced the same problem. After experimentation, Dr. Creger found that chicks often lack vitamin D, and so this nutrient is added to the drinking water.

Buford Welch has real affection for his birds. For the favored pairs of prairie chickens, there are special name plates on the doors of the pens. "My grandchildren named them 'Maude' and 'Charlie' and 'Snoopy' and 'Lucy'." He enjoys raising the chukkars and the quail, but the special pride and feelings are for the prairie chickens. "Oh, yes, they do know me. When the old hen Maude [two years old] sets on her nest, she will peck at me just once if I come too close, but then she just purrs." Welch believes that in spite of being born in captivity, the chickens are still wild birds and could survive if turned loose.

Greening of the Prairies

The month of May is the apex of the spring prairie. Green is taking over, bird song is taking over, insects are taking over. Wildflowers such as golden alexanders, birdsfoot violets, prairie rose, spiderwort, purple milkweed, and ox-eye daisies are taking over. Elizabeth Custer, wife of General George A. Custer, wrote about the flowers she saw in 1867 in her book *Tenting on the Plains:* "The gorgeousness of the reds and oranges of those prairie blossoms was a surprise to me. I had not dreamed that the earth could so glow with rich tints."

The tallgrasses are almost a foot high in some places. Those few wild mammals that have not been exterminated are moving about with new energy, new direction. I try to get a handle on spring; I try to hold on to it.

On my Quivira prairie, I see a deer early one morning. It disappears like a shadow. The hardy scrub oak trees, those indomitable invaders of small island prairies, are leafing out for another year's growth, another year of shading the grasses from the sun, another year of sending out acorns to make more oaks to shade out more grass. Please don't think I am against trees; trees are good for forests. But prairies need fire when trees appear. The only thing that saved my prairie up to now was the practice of intermittent haying in years gone by. And there were accidental wildfires. But slowly like a caged-up wild animal my prairie is changing. The grasses recede a little each year, and the scrub forest ad-

The only thing that saved my prairie up to now was the practice of intermittent haying in years gone by. And there were accidental wildfires. But slowly like a caged-up wild animal my prairie is changing.

Green is taking over, bird song is taking over, insects are taking over. Wildflowers such as golden alexanders, birdsfoot violets, prairie rose, spiderwort, purple milkweed, and ox-eye daisies are taking over.

vances. My Quivira prairie will probably never be missed.

White Cloud

In May I'm on the road again, this time to northeast Kansas, Missouri River country. I am invited to attend Senior Citizens' Craft Day at the Indian Health Center in White Cloud. White Cloud, a nineteenth century river town of 200 people, is nestled in a rare Kansas hardwood forest on the edge of the old Iowa-Sac-Fox Indian Reservation. It was founded in 1856 and soon became a bustling river town of 2,000 people. At one time it was slated to become the largest city in Kansas. Andreas' *History of Kansas* (1883) vividly describes the setting for the town:

The location of White Cloud is an exceptionally beautiful one. In front rolls the smooth expanse of the Missouri, and back of it rise the wooded bluffs with their rich outlines draped in dark foliage. To the north, where the Atchison & Nebraska Railway hugs the sandy cliffs, are fantastic forms that baffle description. Seen from the opposite shore, it looks as if some giant plow had been driven downward to the river in smooth furrows hundreds of feet wide. Farther up, the faces of the bluffs change and present a smooth roundness like the defiant shape of a huge boulder which has lain for centuries on some eastern sea-shore, hurling back the little rollers of a calm summer's day, and emerging shining from the furious lashings of a November gale. It is a picture for an artist, and one which no satiety of mountain or sea-shore can make tame.

The bluffs described are loess bluffs, wild-shaped hardened piles of silt and very fine sand deposited by ancient winds at the time of the glaciers. The name White Cloud is the English translation of *Me-hush-ka,* the name given to several generations of chiefs of the Iowa tribe. The American artists Charles Bird King and George Catlin painted portraits of two generations of White Clouds and their families in the 1820s and 1830s.

When I arrive at the White Cloud Indian Center, the Indian women are already at work making fringed shawls to wear at powwows. Two of the women tell me they are granddaughters of the last Chief White Cloud, James White Cloud, who died in 1940 at the age of 100. A hot lunch is served. It is a good time of work and talk.

Walking the streets of White Cloud is taking steps back in time. The Missouri River dominates the setting. Indeed, the main street runs right into the river without stopping. I am told that the street used to lead to a mammoth riverboat landing in White Cloud's heyday. White Cloud was the place where huge cottonwood logs, "Kansas Mahogany," were unloaded and sawed into timber for shipment west by wagon train to build frontier towns. There are accounts of saw logs piled 2½ stories high and ½ mile long. The old railroad mentioned in Andreas is now a blacktop, but not much else has changed since the early 1900s.

I am introduced to Wolf River Bob (nickname from a nearby stream which runs into the Missouri), purveyor of northeast Kansas history. Bob could pass for Buffalo Bill anytime. His business card reads in part:

WOLF RIVER BOB
Lewis and Clark Trail Guide
Fast Gun—Bullwhips—Western Historian
"Till the Wheels Roll No More"

Bob takes me on a walking tour of several old buildings. Our first stop is Kelley's General Store, housed on the ground floor of the old opera building. Lowell Kelley, in his eightieth year, is a collector of historic paraphernalia pertaining to White Cloud. There are old charts, maps, and photographs of the town. Upstairs the original opera house auditorium is now Kelley's storeroom, and it is an antique-lover's delight. Some of the original opera chairs and even the rolled-up stage curtain are still there. There are fragments of 100-year-old posters on the walls of the ticket booth.

Bob and I continue our walking tour of White Cloud. We visit the old schoolhouse, presently a museum lovingly restored and maintained by the people of White Cloud and a magnificent example of 1870s brick Victorian architecture. We walk on to the Poulet mansion, built in 1858 by Alexis Poulet, the wealthy son of a French Army officer killed in the French Revolution. The house still features the original, fancy cast iron balcony railings shipped up by boat from New Orleans.

It's time for a rest. We sit in a room stacked high with antiques in Bob's house. Bob is talking: "My hair and beard go back to 1959. Before the hippies. I traveled all over the West Coast. I lived in Santa Barbara for quite some time. After working as a missile technician, I went to work on a ranch and helped develop a guest ranch. The fellow didn't have too much money so

I am introduced to Wolf River Bob (nickname from a nearby stream which runs into the Missouri), purveyor of northeast Kansas history. Bob could pass for Buffalo Bill anytime.

that blew that up. Went back to Santa Barbara and put up a wagon camp there. Got together a melodrama show. I would entertain crippled kids. Did some jobs at the movie studios in L.A." I mention that he had to have courage to come back to White Cloud. He replies, "I had courage just to live."

Bob continues: "Did I tell you about the old hotel here? Cyrus McCormick, inventor of the reaper, and R. J. Gatling, who invented the Gatling gun, lived at the hotel. Someone just burned it down a few years ago. They tore down the old Shreve Drug Store too. Said it was an eyesore. There is an element here that doesn't understand what they have. The drugstore was built in the 1850s by a grandson of Colonel Israel Shreve who was with George Washington when he crossed the Delaware. It was the same Shreve family that founded Shreveport, Louisiana."

I take a drive around the area. I stop at the home of Mr. and Mrs. Raymond Frederick on the river front because I am attracted to the nets hanging out to dry, and the wooden fish traps piled on the front yard. The Fredericks are friendly and outgoing. I ask about fishing on the Missouri: "I heard on the radio that the stretch of the river between Omaha to St. Louis is the most polluted stream in the United States. Heck, you'd be surprised at the darn stuff you see in the river. We used to catch a lot of sturgeons, but anymore there're not any sturgeons. There is a few gar. You got to have a special net for the gar. They have all different kinds of nets—wing nets, trammel nets. For catfish you gotta have cheese.

They used to catch catfish that weighed 50 pounds. Those days are gone forever."

Haskell Powwow

I am invited to the May powwow at Haskell Indian Junior College in Lawrence, Kansas, a short drive west. Gail Blake, a Mandan-Arikara from North Dakota and a member of the graduating class, has promised to meet me in one of the teepees set up on campus for the festivities. As I arrive, I see that the parade ground is a kaleidoscope of costumed people. In the center, a great ring of wooden benches with a massive drum to one side has been set up.

The college was founded in 1884 with funds collected from the citizens of Lawrence and matching federal funds. Today there are 1,200 students representing many tribes. The powwow has not begun as Gail and I sit down in the ethereal atmosphere of the teepee, and I tell her of my desire to learn more of the Mandans. Gail begins:

Presently there are about 60 Mandans left—the oldest one just passed away. The Mandans had their own sacred ceremonies. They were the first ones who pierced the skin of the chest and all that. I associate it with the great flood. At one time the earth was flooded. They did another ceremony for growing corn. And they did a buffalo dance. They were the traders of the plains. They even traded with Indians from New Mexico for horses and corn. The Siouxs traded with the Mandans. They had many caches. They dug holes in the ground and buried their corn.

The Mandans are living on the Fort Berthold Indian Reservation, and there are less than 100 full bloods left. My father is a full-blooded

"I heard on the radio that the stretch of the river between Omaha to St. Louis is the most polluted stream in the United States. Heck, you'd be surprised at the darn stuff you see in the river. We used to catch a lot of sturgeons, but anymore there're not any sturgeons."

The location of White Cloud is an exceptionally beautiful one. In front rolls the smooth expanse of the Missouri, and back of it rise the wooded bluffs with their rich outlines draped in dark foliage.

The powwow is like an enormous family reunion. There are songs and dances and greetings for everyone.

My wish is that this drumbeat, these dancers, and this singing could be heard and seen once again out on the prairie.

Mandan. My mom is Arikara. During the time of the 1850s they had a smallpox epidemic, and it just wiped them from the face of the earth. The Gros Ventres and Arikaras suffered too so the three tribes banded together, and they live together to this day. My father is a rancher. He raises cattle. Most of the people up in that area are farmers or ranchers. It's just open prairie—not that many trees.

My grandmother is Annie Eagle. She is almost 100 years old. Two of my aunts speak Mandan really good. None of the children speak Mandan. When my grandfather went to the Christian school, they dropped his Indian name. It was Red Fox. I don't have an Indian name. I could get my Indian name when my mom gets around to it. She has to put up a certain amount of goods. You have to do certain things. She has to give people blankets. She has to cook up a lot of food to feed maybe over a hundred people. She's going to do this. I'm waiting on her.

My grandma gave me my very first blanket. My grandma that's living right now. Before, they used to make everything by hand. It was traditional. But nowadays they come out with all those pretty blankets. A lot of the Indian ladies saw the white ladies with store bought blankets and they wanted them too. Now on the reservation it is a big thing to buy a blanket, especially the Pendletons. They sell for $40. The Indians make their own star quilts. If something is in a store like this the Indians have their own version of it. Remember how the Indians made their own paint from the ground? Now they use fluorescent paint in place of it. And sequins. My own great-grandmother even used sequins on her costume. They use velveteen material too.

Drums beat outside. Gail and I stoop out of the teepee and sit on a blanket by the ring. (The benches are reserved for the dancers.) The powwow is like an enormous family reunion. There are songs and dances and greetings for everyone. There are gourd dances, war dances, round dances, ribbon dances, snake dances, and buffalo dances. There are ribbons, beads, bells, feathers, fans, blankets, rattles, plumes, braids, sequins, and fringes, all shimmer and flash and swirling movement. The drumbeat gives electric life to the dancers like a pounding, racing heart. My wish is that this drumbeat, these dancers, and this singing could be heard and seen once again out on the prairie.

Gail motions a resplendent figure over for introduction. His name is Chebon White Cloud. White Cloud? The same White Cloud family I ask? His answer was all I could hope for:

Yes, I am Otoe-Iowa, First [known] head man [of Iowa Tribe] was Wounded Arrow. His son was the first White Cloud, Iowa they say Me-hush-ka. *His* son was Me-hush-ka number 2; he had the same name. At the agency they enrolled No. 2 as Francis White Cloud. Then Jim White Cloud was his youngest son. He [Francis] had another older son named Jefferson. Uncle Jefferson got killed in Oklahoma. He became chief of the Ioways in Oklahoma when they moved down there. Grandpa Jim [as mentioned previously, born 1840] stayed up with the northern ones. Then Grandpa Jim had two wives. Indian way. His first wife, he chose to live with her when the allotment act came in. His second wife was Sally Deroine. She's my great-great-grandmother. She moved with her two children to Oklahoma when the allotment act came in. And my great-grandpa's name was Robert White Cloud [Sally's son]. Grandpa Bob also had an older half-brother named Louis. Louis was Grandpa Jim's first son by his first wife.

There are gourd dances, war dances, round dances, ribbon dances, snake dances, and buffalo dances. There are ribbons, beads, bells, feathers, fans, blankets, rattles, plumes, braids, sequins, and fringes, all shimmer and flash and swirling movement.

This is where the White Cloud, Kansas ones come from—the northern ones. Our bunch stayed in Oklahoma. We passed the chieftainship on to Uncle Louis, but he died, and he had a son named Daniel White Cloud, and he died in 1970 in Oklahoma. His elder son's name is Jimmy, and he had another son named Bo, but he wasn't really a White Cloud, he was adopted. Old man Daniel raised him. Now before Grandpa Jim died he passed his chieftain's clothes to his only son living; that was Grandpa Bob. Now out of the family heirlooms there was Grandpa Jim's bearclaw necklace, and it has been gone from my side of the family for some twenty-five years. I have it now. It was just returned to me. Now Grandpa Bob when he died he had one son, Theodore, my grandfather. My father's name is Douglas White Cloud. I'm the eldest of his children. That's my genealogy.

Otoes and Iowas are the same people. Otoes, Ioways and Missouris are same people. We ruled east of the Missouri. There was also another faction—Omahas, Poncas, Osages, and Kaws [Kansas], and they ruled the west. One time we were all allies against the Sioux. And, of course, later on most of us moved to Oklahoma. Our names also happen to mean The People—People Up the River, People By the River, People of the Muddy River, People Down the River. That's what our names mean. These other names they gave us—Otoes, Iowa, Missouri, these stuck. But we call ourselves The People, The First People. I have an uncle. He's M.C. of the powwow. He's the last living tribal historian of the Otoes. He knows our family history. He knows that I am descended from that old Chief White Cloud.

We were a proudful nation. We stopped the Sioux dead in their tracks. Otoes were a small tribe but were such fierce fighters. We fought to the last man. We wouldn't give up. Either we came home victorious, or we died on the battlefield.

Catlin painted my great-great-great-Grandfather. He painted his wife too.

The drums and singing continue louder than ever, and I am thinking that the White Cloud family is a good candidate for a new version of *Roots*. White Cloud continues:

Very few of the young people know how to put on a powwow. They are just like the white people. They are just there to look on. I have a culture; I have a heritage. I have chieftain's blood. Nowadays we have no more chiefs. A lot of people depend on grandma and grandpa to tell them the old ways. One day they'll wake up and grandma and grandpa will no longer be there, and they'll be lost. They're truly lost. They're still Indian, but they will have nothing.

There are old men on the reservation who know more than I do. They don't like to boast or brag. That's not the Indian way. We had a White Cloud chief's song but that is lost now. Many people have heard of it, but they can't remember it.

There are very few white people who come among us who have a true heart. What little I know of my people, it's going. It will be gone. I want to die before this happens. These young ones, they don't understand.

"We had a White Cloud chief's song but that is lost now. Many people have heard of it, but they can't remember it."

YEAR OF THE PRAIRIE
SUMMER

Rodeo

A tallgrass prairie summer after a long spring begins to be warm, but it gives us collateral: it is also rich with human, plant, and animal activity. Go to any county in any of the prairie states, and you will find a rodeo or a parade, or both—or the promise of one somewhere in the vicinity. Parades are joyous events, and I want to see all of them. A parade is a white man's powwow. The prairie town's main street is one continual stage with the clean-cut, frontier-style stone storefronts as a backdrop. There are two groups of parade participants: the marchers-riders and the spectators. There is little to distinguish one from the other; they are symbiotic. Dress for a parade is strictly western. If you have even one item of western attire, you must wear it to the parade.

At Cottonwood Falls, a singular town of the Flint Hills, during the first weekend in June the brick main street is festooned with banners, bunting, flags, and posters. My parade this day begins with a cadre of motorcycle policemen followed by a small contingent of uniformed soldiers. Then comes the high school band and after that a plethora of horses and riders dressed to the nines. A cacophonous mixture of more bands, more horses, and more floats follows—a 4-H float, a Vacation Bible School float, Boy Scout and Girl Scout floats, an American Legion float, a turkey red wheat float. (Alas, there is no big bluestem float or prairie wildflower float or buffalo float.) There are horse-drawn wagons, antique cars, bicycles, tricycles, tractors, and massive silver-cabbed cattle trucks with ear-drum-splitting air-horns honking a discordant cadenza to the entire performance. When all of this has gone by, I want to run ahead of it with the children and watch it all over again.

After the parade there is nothing to do but mill around with the rest of the crowd until the rodeo begins. The rodeo grounds are shoulder-to-shoulder people with intermittent groupings of every kind of horse trailer under the sun. Horses are groomed

Dress for a parade is strictly western. If you have even one item of western attire, you must wear it to the parade.

Go to any county in any of the prairie states, and you will find a rodeo or a parade, or both—or the promise of one somewhere in the vicinity.

At Cottonwood Falls, a singular town of the Flint Hills, during the first weekend in June the brick main street is festooned with banners, bunting, flags, and posters.

The sun is low over the enveloping bright green Flint Hills. We settle into our grandstand seats for an evening of cowboys doing their thing.

and pampered and loved. Cumbrous Brahma bulls in pens await their moment in the ring as do the other bovine creatures brought in for this occasion. The music of Bing the King, "Have Organ, Will Travel," is heard over the loudspeaker. The sun is low over the enveloping bright green Flint Hills. We settle into our grandstand seats for an evening of cowboys doing their thing.

Wheat Harvest

Wheat. Some say it is the most beautiful word in the English language. Wheat is worshipped on the prairie. In June the eyes, minds, pocketbooks, and stomachs of the world are on the wheat belt, carved out of the original prairie. My son Don, who is to be my assistant for summer prairie photography, and I set out to find the wheat harvest. The long caravans of custom wheat harvesters have finished their work in the southern wheat states, Texas and Oklahoma, and are, according to the *Kansas City Star*, working into the southern counties of Kansas. We head straight south and stop for lunch and a tour of Fort Scott, now being restored by the National Park Service. Established in 1842, Fort Scott, which is roughly equidistant from Fort Leavenworth, Kansas, and Fort Smith, Arkansas, was initially an outpost for peace keeping along the border between Indian and white territory. The fort area became a civilian community during the "Bleeding Kansas" years just before the Civil War and was reactivated during the war as a staging area for Union troops. It again was active during the great westward expansion and

down on it, even on the hottest days, it is always damp and cool, like air conditioning. Steve continues: "This coolness on the ground has to attract the nesting birds. It's a difficult concept to get across—that native grass is so much more beneficial. The public looks for a simple, concise explanation about the prairie. You just can't explain how the prairie works in short easy steps."

I mention a chance meeting on a plane to Washington, D.C. with a Missouri congressman. The congressman was very nice, very friendly, but totally unaware of prairie preservation attempts in Missouri, or in any other state. I wonder what steps are necessary to be taken to educate both politicians and the public about the importance of our Midwest life support system.

Steve comments: "We're still in an era when the environment is not understood. Saving a wild area is still anti-progress. We had prairie on our farm in Montgomery County, Kansas, on my Dad's land. I knew it had to have been prairie, and I wanted to see it come back. Then as I got hired on by the Kansas Fish and Game Department as a professional, the prairie grew on me. The more you know about it, the more you want to know. It really grows. You can study it a lifetime. We're still in our infancy."

Don, Steve, and I walk over to Taberville Prairie. Steve continues: "Taberville is hayed annually between July 1 and July 15. The reason you see so many flowers here as opposed to mostly grass on the Kansas prairies is that haying preserves many of the flowering plants that are eaten and

A prairie is a place where hundreds of plants and animals can exist together in harmony—something man cannot do. Several of these species are the forefathers of the cultivated plants we have today. Many of them possess medical properties that we don't yet understand. A number of them may be used in the future to solve many of our problems—such as cancer.

The coming of the wheat seed in the little baskets of the Mennonites changed the prairies forever. One group came to central Kansas in the early 1870s, and each family brought seed wheat with them, mostly a strain called "turkey red."

Photo courtesy of Don Duncan

eventually wiped out by cattle. For the last twenty-five years Taberville has been managed by haying or mowing. Now we are learning more about fire, but up until the last year or two, Missouri has been anti-fire because of all the forests. We are going to start using more fire and more [cattle] grazing because our research is showing that we need all three techniques to give us the highest diversity of plants and animals."

This is the first time I hear about cattle being allowed on a wild prairie. I ask whether cattle are really allowed on state owned prairies. Steve answers: "Yes. Our studies show that both underuse and overuse result in the least diversity. It must be somewhere in the middle."

I ask whether buffalo graze differently than cattle. Steve answers that buffalo graze much more efficiently. "A buffalo is an eating machine. He eats everything, whereas a cow will pick and choose. But we can't utilize buffalo because of management problems."

I ask: "What would you say to the person that said to you 'Why all the fuss about native grass? Why not plant fescue?'" Steve feels strongly on this matter.

Biologically speaking, fescue is something that is totally foreign to our wildlife. They can't adapt to it. It's so aggressive that it's sterile. Birds use it very little for nesting—or foraging. You would think that grass is grass to animals, and this thought lulls people into a false sense of security. In the settlement of the United States, the Europeans brought many plants with them. The native plants—the European didn't know how to manage, so they were in his way. He

began eliminating them and replacing them with European strains. Just in the last twenty years we are beginning to realize what we have—what nature has been providing for thousands of years. You notice here that everyone is harvesting fescue. It's just taken Missouri by storm. Cattle don't like fescue, but they will eat it as a last resort. Fescue hasn't taken over yet in Kansas. It scares me. I grew up when it was just getting started in southeast Kansas. I never knew what it could do, how thoroughly it could choke out everything until I came to Missouri. Just a matter of time in Kansas too.

Don and I camp out for the night in the nearby Schell-Osage Campground. It's a good night's sleep, and we awake to many bird sounds. We pack up camp and meet Tom Toney, the Missouri State Prairie Biologist, at a minuscule prairie called "Little Savannah." It is a sea of blacksampson and butterflies. Tom tells us: "This prairie had a spring burn and will have a spring burn next year. The dominant flora here is purple cone flower or blacksampson, the orange one is butterfly milkweed. There is wild petunia, lead plant, goatsrue, black-eyed susan, and coreopsis, and compass plant is just coming into bloom."

Tom takes us for a ride in his pickup truck to some of the other prairies, and he tells us more as he drives:

We are now at the Wa-Kon-Tah Prairie, a Nature Conservancy prairie. The name is Osage Indian. It is 630 acres. There are these three Conservancy prairies within 1½ miles: the other two are Moko Prairie which is 416 acres and Montigall, 188 acres.

There is no doubt that the hayer preserved the prairies we have left. Missouri was one of the hay capitals of the world. It was shipped to

We pack up camp and meet Tom Toney, the Missouri State Prairie Biologist, at a minuscule prairie called "Little Savannah." It is a sea of blacksampson and butterflies.

Just in the last twenty years we are beginning to realize what we have—what nature has been providing for thousands of years.

On following pages.
The full, round, milk white globe appears over a pinkish-glazed sky, and for a few magic moments setting sun and rising moon face each other as they have done monthly since the time the earth began.

Kentucky for the race horses. Since World War II, the high cost of hay transportation has brought about a change in land use. From an economic point of view the farmers had to go to a bean crop—a cultivated crop.

A prairie is a place where hundreds of plants and animals can exist together in harmony—something man cannot do. Several of these species are the forefathers of the cultivated plants we have today. Many of them possess medical properties that we don't yet understand. A number of them may be used in the future to solve many of our problems—such as cancer. We could learn from them about drought resistance, not to mention peace of mind and beauty. The prairies are a refuge from the modern world.

Prairie Night

There is still time in June for Don and me to take an extended camping trip to the Konza prairie. The night before a camping trip to the Konza I lie awake for hours thinking about what I will do when I get out there. I am anticipating the full moon (it is three-quarters full now) and thinking about technical things and aesthetic things. I have just read a piece on Lilo Raymond, who, I believe, is my kind of photographer. She started in her thirties as I did and puts good words together about the first five years. "The first five years are pure joy, and then you are really hooked, and you know you can never cease learning, studying, running, literally, to the darkroom to find out what you have done."

In prairie country the best photographs are taken in early morning when the light is crisp and clean. The colors shine out defined and clear in the slanted rays of the rising sun. You might as well forget it during the whole middle of the day. By then, the sun has gathered unconquerable strength and beats down bleaching out this bare bones earth. At noonday everything runs for cover, including wise photographers, because no matter what you do, the pictures tend to come out overexposed. Life and color emerge again late in the afternoon.

We pick a June-perfect day, a day of racing clouds and their running shadows making the whole landscape shimmer across our field of vision. We meet Dr. Lloyd Hulbert at the old Dewey Ranch headquarters, and he takes us on a "jeep trail" tour of this portion of the Konza that I have never seen except for my brief encounter with the prairie chickens in the spring. Don and I must count ourselves fortunate to have as our guide one of the most well informed prairie scientists in the world, who is also a friend. There are high hopes, he tells us, for the Konza that include introducing bison, elk, and antelope, updating and improving the old, but solid, stone ranch house as a prairie research center, the purchase of improved fire control equipment, and many other things.

This time we choose a spot for our camp along a stream that is thick with ancient oaks. On a walk I am in waist-high weeds in an area that had been plowed, but as I climb into the open hills, the grasses are healthy again. There are rocks and grasshoppers, squirrels, a raccoon, and a coyote. There are dickcissels, red-winged blackbirds, and mourning doves. The male red-winged

There are high hopes for the Konza that include introducing bison, elk, and antelope, updating and improving the old, but solid, stone ranch house as a prairie research center, the purchase of improved fire control equipment, and many other things.

On a walk I am in waist-high weeds in an area that had been plowed, but as I climb into the open hills, the grasses are healthy again. There are rocks and grasshoppers, squirrels, a raccoon, and a coyote.

When it is too dark to take pictures, Don and I go back to the tent; the campsite is bathed in the long twilight of moonlight and fading sunlight, and we sleep.

We cannot see the herd from our tent so we drive through the gate to the grazing area, and there they are. They surround the Blazer, and it is unnerving to be so close to such enormous, unpredictable, and curious animals.

blackbirds perch on anything and act like they own the prairie. There are prairie waters springing from rain saturated grass roots, oozing out of the earth, and running down the brown cowpaths. There are huge, pocked boulders lying along the stream where we camp. Some of the old oaks seem to grow right out of the rocks, their trunks and roots shaped weirdly. The sky is all over everything.

It is time for the full moon to rise. I walk through the grass and flowers to a high hill and wait. The full, round, milk white globe appears over a pinkish-glazed sky, and for a few magic moments setting sun and rising moon face each other as they have done monthly since the time the earth began.

When it is too dark to take pictures, Don and I go back to the tent; the campsite is bathed in the long twilight of moonlight and fading sunlight, and we sleep. We sleep; the moon never leaves us for an instant, and it shines right through the tent. The killdeers finally stop darting at us, the quail stop their calling. It is another prairie night, and I own the moon and the stars.

Morning comes as the moon sinks down right on the hills. Heavy dew is on the grass, on everything. I race up the hill chasing the moon before I can get my eyes fully open. I go as high as I am able before it sinks below the far line of the earth. With the sun safely up and the moon secured behind the hills, I rush back to finish my sleep.

Where the Buffalo Roam

Summer wears on to July. The tallgrasses are at least waist high. Eastern gamagrass, that ancient "granddad" of grasses that some scientists say is related to corn, is seeded out with hairy tassels. The other tallgrasses will take more time.

No account of the prairie would be complete without some kind of narrative of the buffalo, that ancient prairie creature once described by Cortez as having "a hunch on its Back like a Camel; its Flanks dry, its tail large, and its Neck covered with Hair like a Lion; It is cloven footed, its Head armed like that of a Bull, which it resembles in fierceness, with no less strength and agility." There are several small, private buffalo herds in Kansas—a small group at Ft. Riley near Junction City and one or two state owned herds. The largest herd is at the Maxwell Game Preserve in McPherson County. The 2,560-acre preserve was deeded to the state in 1944 by Henry Irving Maxwell with the stipulation that it stay forever in its natural state and be a refuge for wildlife. The buffalo herd averages two hundred head, and the elk herd numbers about fifty.

Don and I arrive at Maxwell late on a July day and set up our camp at the adjacent McPherson County State Lake. As we drive back through the preserve, we do not see the elusive buffalo or elk, but we do notice the high wire fence. It is at least eight feet tall, and we are glad it stands between our camp and the buffalo.

The next morning we awake to a God-awful sound. It is the primeval grunting-snort of the buffalo. We cannot see the herd from our tent so we drive through the gate to the grazing area, and there they are. They surround the Blazer, and it is unnerv-

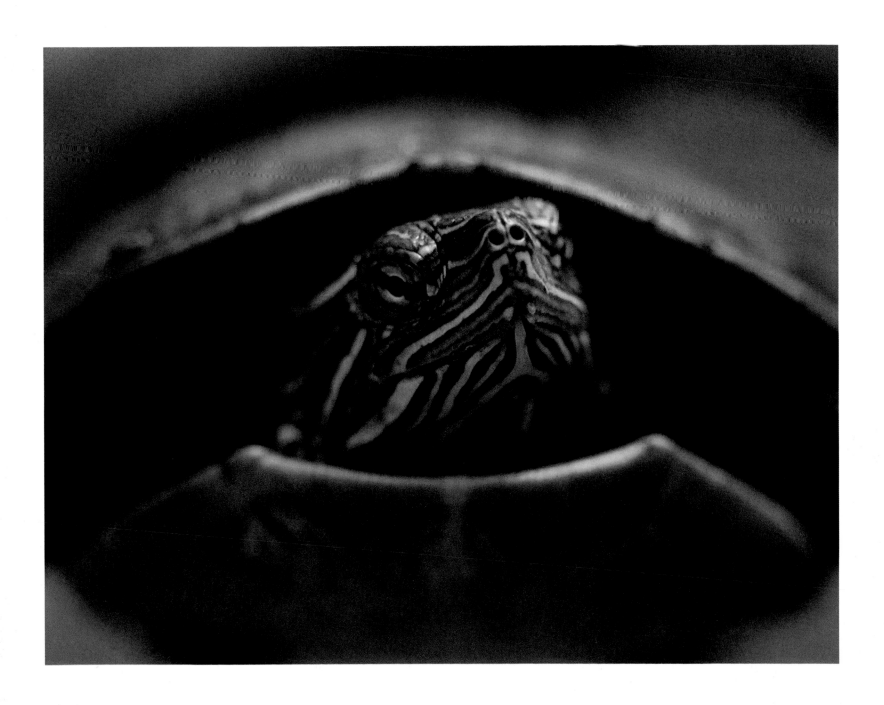

were selected from seven potential sites meeting park service criteria. All seven sites are thoroughly evaluated in the Prairie National Park Planning Directive written by a park service study team. This planning directive states the purpose and objectives of a prairie national park:

Prairie National Park should be a reserve for the preservation of an unimpaired population of native plants and animals, a place where future generations can see what the historic tallgrass prairie was like, and the prairie's significance as a unique natural resource can be communicated. However, equally important and perhaps more readily comprehended is the prairie's cultural role—its influence on human development in America from prehistoric to contemporary times. The significance of the prairie to native Americans and early pioneers, to sodbusters and cowboys, to small homesteaders and great combines, and even to people who have never called the prairie their home—this is what will engage visitors and encourage them to explore further. Hence, the purpose of a Prairie National Park can be seen as twofold: to preserve and protect a relatively undisturbed portion of the natural prairie environment, and to interpret its role in shaping America.

There are six main points outlined as criteria for prairie parklands:

1. A representative tallgrass prairie ecosystem illustrating characteristic topography, vegetation, drainage patterns, and wildlife.
2. A tallgrass prairie community that is relatively stable or in the process of succession to a natural condition, as demonstrated by a relative lack of disturbances and invader species, vigor of plant communities, and predominance of climax vegetation.
3. An area that manifests the scenic attributes of the prairie—spaciousness, expansive grasslands, riparian woodlands, and rolling topography.
4. A manageable unit that permits effective control and protection of resources, that encompasses either complete watersheds or headwaters, that encloses an area with more or less equal dimensions, and that lacks interruptive features.
5. A site that can be adapted to provide numerous and diverse opportunities for visitor enjoyment of natural, cultural, and scenic values within a natural tallgrass prairie setting.
6. A land area that is relatively free of adverse man-made intrusions or disturbances.

The STP site selection committee followed the park service guidelines in most instances during its own evaluation. The unanimous choice of the committee is the Chase South site. Lawrence R. Wagner writes of the decision in his report to the STP Board of Counselors:

The tallgrass prairie covered so much country from east to west and from north to south that it probably is impossible to define a "typical" tallgrass prairie. The flat lands of northern Illinois with their vast, unbroken stretches of grass and forbs; the rolling hills of southern Wisconsin with their boreal savannahs; the pot-hole wetland prairies of southern Minnesota, northern Iowa, and South Dakota; the rolling prairies of southern Iowa and northern Missouri; the very gently rolling lands of eastern North and South Dakota, Nebraska, and Kansas; the Cross Timber savannahs of Oklahoma and Texas. The tallgrass prairie was these and more. . . .
One can't put all these areas in a blender and produce one that is "typical." One *can* say with a certain degree of assurance that the major part

The STP site selection committee followed the park service guidelines in most instances during its own evaluation. The unanimous choice of the committee is the Chase South site.

Farther on there is the sickening sight of a slaughtered coyote strung up on a barbed wire fence. What makes man so misguided? Coyotes are infinitely more beautiful and useful alive in the landscape.

There is a crumbling schoolhouse in the distance, and we drive over to it. The "students" are young steers playing endless follow-the-leader through a hole in the rear wall and out the front door.

of the original tallgrass prairie region had three things in common: (1) tall grasses; (2) deep soils; and (3) vastness.

To me, these are the hallmarks that should characterize a tallgrass prairie national park. The deep soils of the Chase South site make the tallgrasses possible, and the wide vistas this land provides gives me the feeling of vastness to a degree unmatched by the other two sites. And I can truly believe for a moment that I, with my dependent family and my meager belongings, have just emigrated from the forests of eastern North America and here I stand, unprotected by their sheltering boughs and unfettered by their horizon destroying limitations. Here I can be, for that instant, a Westering man. I can know his fears because I feel them. I can know his stirring response to vastness as goose flesh dots my skin. I feel my heritage and I am proud and glad.

Don and I drive southwest through Emporia, the hometown of famed editor and writer William Allen White, to Strong City, a community on the edge of the Chase South site. We check into the Flint Hills Motel just after lunch. The day is dismal so we decide to take an afternoon nap before exploring the backroads. When we come to life again, there is still little hope of good light so we stop at the Wagon Wheel Cafe for an early dinner. Don consumes the largest T-bone steak I have ever seen.

We take an after dinner drive south on the state-designated "Prairie Parkway." This parkway follows State Highway 177 north and south through the Flint Hills. The Kansas Highway Department has marked the route, but the state legislature as yet has done nothing to protect the scenic quality of the corridor.

Because there is not enough time before dark to tour the actual park site, we turn left near the next small town, Bazaar, and we travel until the road is blocked by a rancher's gate. This is one of the most beautiful spots we yet have seen. This evening the hills disclose the silence that is their hallmark. They lie here in the mist like some huge body covered with a soft green quilt.

The next morning it is raining. We eat again at the Wagon Wheel, which is brimful of men wearing their western hats and work clothes. The town priest is here, a rotund, happy man dressed in black shirt and pants and no hat. This sets him apart. The conversation is about growing tomatoes and a recent prairie wildfire. I order a "flat," which is one huge pancake that laps over the plate.

It is still raining after breakfast, but prairie skies are always dramatic after a rain. Don and I start out hoping for the best. We drive south again toward Chase South. Just past Cassoday, known as the Prairie Chicken Capital of the World, we turn left on a dirt road and intend to make a big circle through the site. The sky commences clearing as we had hoped, and we bounce and slide sideways in the mud. We are engulfed in that fine, fresh light breaking out that turns everything chartreuse after a summer prairie rain. We watch a rainbow form and re-form, and there is a great urge to run over to the hill where we think we can see the end of it.

This land is cut off from the world. It is wild, primitive, beautiful. Big bluestem grows in healthy roadside clumps, and

compass plants are blooming. We take pictures of two kinds of turtles and many birds perching on the fence posts for lack of anything better to do. There is a crumbling schoolhouse in the distance, and we drive over to it. The "students" are young steers playing endless follow-the-leader through a hole in the rear wall and out the front door. Farther on there is the sickening sight of a slaughtered coyote strung up on a barbed wire fence. What makes man so misguided? Coyotes are infinitely more beautiful and useful alive in the landscape.

We drive all day making our circle tour, then return to the turnpike and head home full of thoughts that the fate of all this life, all this beauty, lies in the hands of a few men and women in Congress.

Prairie Wedding

Artie Lucas, a friend from northeast Kansas, has invited me to his outdoor prairie wedding, and how can I refuse? July swelters as we drive onto the appointed farm pasture in Brown County. Many guests are enjoying themselves swimming in the pond, picnicking, smoking "grass," and listening to rock music blaring from loud speakers. The bride, Nancy, is changing into the wedding dress that she herself has made, and someone places a garland of prairie flowers in her hair. Artie takes her hand and leads her down by the pond where the minister waits to begin the ceremony.

Artie, the groom, welcomes the guests: "As some of you know, we've lived together three years, and we feel like we're already married in our own hearts. So

"We've chosen today to be married not only to each other but also to join our two families into one. We'd like you to stay and celebrate with us. Got lots of food, drinks, nice prairie pond to do some swimming in."

we've chosen today to be married not only to each other but also to join our two families into one. We'd like you to stay and celebrate with us. Got lots of food, drinks, nice prairie pond to do some swimming in. To us, marriage is the art of loving, learning and living harmoniously with each other. . . . With this ring of love and happiness I give my love to you forever."

The bride responds: "We've shared a lot of things these last three years, and I want to go on sharing with Artie. There's been a lot of ups and downs but a lot of living and learning and growing, and it has made us stronger as one, and I feel secure in the fact that our love will continue to grow, and I give willingly of myself and my love to strengthen our marriage through trust and sensitivity—and I love you!"

Artie, excited and restless, can contain himself no longer. "Give me some of that pig." (There is a whole roast pig cooking over an open fire.) But the minister has not yet had his say. "I think that is what life is all about—its relationships, its loving, its caring, caring in a greater family which involves all of you and in this family relationship which you've established. You've pledged yourselves each to the other sometime back, and you're reaffirming that now. I think we're reaffirming our love for you. That is what life is about— love, relationships, having a good time, spreading joy and making the world a better place to live. These two are doing that, and we're grateful to them. I pronounce you husband and wife together." Nancy says "Right on!" and Artie yells "Yah hoo! Let's go swimming!"

On this evening the clouds are performing for us.

In the potholes that still hold water we see hundreds of resident ducks, geese, and herons.

On preceding pages:

There is an incredible thick white mist accenting the still black silhouette upon silhouette of the hills. The sun blazes the sky into stripes of orange and gold, and then the mist itself becomes a pink reflection of the sky. It is a magic land.

Ordway Prairie

It is August. This is the month prairie people wait for. Everything is in climax. The height of the flowering plants follows the height of the grasses. Sunflowers, prairie dock, gayfeather, rattlesnake master, goldenrod, and asters are coloring the prairies. The grasses already hint at their fall plumage. there are golds, yellows, even maroon and purple appearing on grass leaves.

Don and I are driving north toward South Dakota to visit the Samuel H. Ordway Memorial Prairie, a Nature Conservancy prairie second in size only to the Konza. We follow the Missouri River to Sioux City, Iowa, and notice that native grass, even along the fences, is completely wiped out, and there are few sunflowers. All the land has been plowed. As we reach South Dakota, the land flattens. There are prosperous-looking farms, and all the barns are painted red with white trim. On this particular August day, the clouds are spaced across the immense sky in elongated puffs, and these puffs serve to heighten the spacial feeling of the land.

The land begins to roll gently, then becomes bumpy. This is the Coteau du Missouri, a range of hills that is another legacy of the extensive action of the most recent glacier. It is a rough, rocky area similar to the Flint Hills. We turn west toward Aberdeen, South Dakota, and then proceed northwest to the Ordway Prairie. The manager, Paul Bultsma, is there to greet us. We accept his offer to stay in the bunkhouse and move our gear inside. In the bunkhouse kitchen we sip coffee, and I

skim the maps and brochures Paul has given me. I read that the Ordway Prairie covers 7,600 acres and was purchased by the Nature Conservancy in 1975. It was named after Samuel H. Ordway, a founder of the Conservation Foundation and an author of several conservation books.

Like the Konza, the land rolls, but here it rolls more gently. Ordway, too, was saved from the plow by its rockiness. It lies on the edge of the Coteau du Missouri and was once a part of the rich hunting grounds of the Sioux. It is just out of the tallgrass area so it is in the shifting, transition area known as midgrass prairie. There are grasses unfamiliar to me such as whitetop, spikerush, needle and thread, porcupine grass, and on the dry summits of some of the hills, buffalo grass from the shortgrass prairie. There are no running streams. Water on the land comes from over 400 glacial potholes of all sizes, and at this time many of them are dry due to a summer-long drought.

Don and I reconnoiter the prairie by driving the perimeter gravel road shown on our map. From this road we can look across the prairie and see that is it more delicate, more refined than the Konza, and it also seems more remote. Indeed, there are less than a million people in all of South Dakota. We try to take pictures of two rodent-like animals burrowing in the middle of the road, and later Paul tells us that these are probably Richardson's ground squirrels. In the potholes that still hold water we see hundreds of resident ducks, geese, and herons.

Upon our return to the bunkhouse, we

There is something to photograph at every step, in every direction.

share a quick dinner with several other prairie researchers, and we meet Paul and his wife for a long hike to the highest spot on the prairie. (Walking and horseback riding only are allowed at Ordway.) On this evening the clouds are performing for us. In spite of the rocks, which Paul tells us are white quartz and granite, the hills are easier to climb, and the plants daintier than the Konza's. Big bluestem is plentiful, but it grows in miniature, and it has turned a deep wine red. Little bluestem, too, is abundant, and it is rusty bronze. There are several kinds of sunflowers blooming, and not a tree in sight.

The clouds billow and begin to be spectacular. We flush a jackrabbit, and he lopes off in front of us. It is my first look at a jackrabbit, and he seems as big as a coyote. His antenna ears can be seen forever across the hills. The sunset is one of those rare good ones. We sit on the highest hill without talking, feeling the breeze and the wonder of the evening.

I am up the next morning before daylight. I pack up the cameras and the "Off" spray—South Dakota gnats seem fond of the back of my neck—for a long hike. Don is sleeping in but has promised to cook a big breakfast when I return. As I leave the bunkhouse, I cannot decide which way to go: toward the big pothole lake and the birds or toward the high hill and the splendid vistas. The rising sun does not wait for me to decide so I must set up the tripod then and there. There is an incredible thick white mist accenting the still black silhouette upon silhouette of the hills. The sun blazes the sky into stripes of orange and gold, and then the mist itself becomes a pink reflection of the sky. It is a magic land.

My walk is a long one. There is something to photograph at every step, in every direction. The sun is high and hot when I return to the bunkhouse. Don says, "I thought you were lost," and in a sense I was.

In the afternoon there is another hike and more discoveries. I get to the pothole lake this time, but in my excitement I move too quickly and spook the birds. There is no hiding place in this country! The next morning I successfully stalk the birds on hands and knees with the long lens, don't ask me how, and come away with many pictures. A black crowned night heron is especially cooperative.

Willa Cather's Prairie

We must leave Ordway the next morning and head south toward Nebraska and home. I have chosen a little traveled highway that will take us through the famed sand hill country of Nebraska. The wild sand hills have been tamed by the plow in many places and are now covered with neat rows of corn or giant sunflowers from Eurasia. We travel through Grand Island, across the silent Platte, empty now of its sandhill cranes, and on to Red Cloud, home of author Willa Cather and the Willa Cather Memorial Prairie. Red Cloud, named after the great Sioux chief, is another clean-cut prairie town left over from the nineteenth century. It is Sunday morning and so both the Willa Cather Museum and the Cather home are not open for our inspection. The Cather Memorial Prairie is just south of town at the Kansas border. As we drive into the loop entry, the sky begins to run dark and low over the land as if Cather herself set the mood for our coming. Her beloved red grass surrounds us.

On the marker we read that the prairie is 610 acres and was purchased by the Nature Conservancy in 1974 with funds from the Woods Charitable Fund. We read that Willa Cather came to Nebraska in 1883 at the age of nine from the more civilized country of Virginia. She later wrote of her early impressions of the wild prairie: "This country was mostly wild pasture and as naked as the back of your hand. I was little and homesick and lonely and my mother was homesick and nobody paid any attention to us. So the country and I had it out together and by the end of the first autumn, that shaggy grass country had gripped me with a passion I have never been able to shake. It has been the happiness and curse of my life."

The wild sand hills have been tamed by the plow in many places and are now covered with neat rows of corn or giant sunflowers from Eurasia.

"So the country and I had it out together and by the end of the first autumn, that shaggy grass country had gripped me with a passion I have never been able to shake. It has been the happiness and curse of my life."

We observe many wildflowers:
cardinal flower, coreopsis, foxglove,
bottle gentian, and the uncommon
Riddell's goldenrod.

YEAR OF THE PRAIRIE
FALL

Eastern Prairies

Summer and happy August are over, and both sons must be off to college. The decision is made that Herb and I will drive with Don to his school in Maine. (David, our elder son, is a student at this time at Kansas University.) We plan our return from the east via three or four preserved prairies in Ohio, Indiana, and Illinois.

Our first prairie stop toward home is Toledo, Ohio. We had arranged to meet Jeanne Hawkins, a deeply involved prairie preservation person, at the 120-acre Irwin Prairie just west of the city. Irwin lies in an area of oak openings in the northwestern Ohio dunes region, and it is less than twenty miles from the shore of Lake Erie. It is within an area of deep sand lying over a layer of hard blue clay. As recently as the 1830s, the area was part of an enormous swamp called Black Swamp, and portions of the land were underwater most of the time. When the early white settlers arrived, they tried to drain the swamp for farming but at the time only succeeded in making the land usable for intermittent haying.

Our visit to Irwin Prairie in early September is during a dry period, and the low sandy areas are covered with a mid-height sedge called twigbrush, a lush, green grass-like plant. We observe many wildflowers: cardinal flower, coreopsis, foxglove, bottle gentian, and the uncommon Riddell's goldenrod. Jeanne tells us that several kinds of rare moths and butterflies are found here as well as the spotted turtle and the eastern garter snake.

The accounts of the preservation of the "saved" prairies seem to have a number of basic steps in common, and Irwin Prairie is no exception. Most prairies that have been saved were protected from the plow or bulldozer because of some natural impediment, and then a citizen or group of citizens sooner or later becomes involved in an effort to save them. This effort must center around both money and politics, for like it or not, local, state, and federal laws are the only real protection for a piece of land. A private owner may have the best of intentions but is powerless by himself.

Irwin Prairie began to be noticed in the

Our visit to Irwin Prairie in early September is during a dry period, and the low sandy areas are covered with a mid-height sedge called twigbrush, a lush, green grass-like plant.

1920s, but money was not raised until the 1960s when a group of people including Jeanne Hawkins formed the Northwest Ohio Open Space Trust Fund. This group began to work with the Nature Conservancy, and this in turn generated more funds. Later on in the early 1970s, the Ohio state legislature began to be aware of its natural treasures and passed the Ohio Scenic Rivers Bill and the Ohio Natural Areas Bill. At the same time, the Ohio State Department of Natural Resources was gaining more power, and, finally, Irwin was purchased from the Nature Conservancy and is now a part of the Ohio Natural Areas System.

With Jeanne we also visit a smaller, but equally interesting prairie just a few miles away, the twenty-six-acre Schwamberger Prairie. Its value had long been known, but the desire to save it intensified after an accidental fire in 1971 which triggered the blooming of suppressed wildflowers, among them twenty different kinds of orchids. Schwamberger Prairie also is covered with native wild blueberries and strawberries, once a great source of food for the Indians, big and little bluestem, indiangrass, and many other kinds of plants.

The next stop on our trip home is the Hoosier Prairie in Hammond, Indiana, and there is a remarkable prairie person to greet us here also, Irene Herlocker. It is a poignant occasion. Irene's husband, Bob, passed away suddenly the night before our meeting, but Irene insists on seeing us. She explains: "This is our favorite place in all the world. Bob's photography helped preserve this place. It took ten years of our

lives. He was looking forward to meeting you, and he would want me to be here. I am planning to scatter his ashes over the prairie."

Hoosier is the only preserved public prairie in Indiana. There are just no other prairies of any size left in the state. In 1975 the Indiana legislature, realizing its importance, voted to put $1,000,000 into the state budget to purchase it. It is 330 acres in size and contains over 300 kinds of plants, at least 43 of them quite rare in Indiana. Hoosier Prairie represents the prime example of the grand prairie, the prairie peninsula which formed the eastern boundary of the deciduous forest in northwestern Indiana. It is the first truly urban prairie I have seen and is surrounded by telephone poles and wires, by all manner of city sprawl. It is in the Calumet region of Indiana which is known for its steel mills and oil refineries. A more unlikely place for a stretch of wild prairie you would not find.

Just a short drive west to suburban Chicago takes us to our next "eastern" prairie, the 120-acre Markham Prairie in Cook County, Illinois, and just forty-five minutes south of the Loop. This prairie contains more than 250 plant species in its varied topography of alkaline fen, wet prairie and mesic prairie. The regal fritallary butterfly, rare in the Chicago area, is found here.

The "godfather" of Markham Prairie is Karl Bartel. We are fortunate to arrive at the prairie on a Sunday morning during a regular lecture-tour from the Field Museum. Karl is talking to half the tour group, and Phil Hanson from the museum is talking to the other half. Karl tells us that the prairie was in a flood plain after the last glacier receded and was part of a sandbar that paralleled the shoreline of Lake Michigan. The history of its use includes sheep grazing after the first settlers arrived in the 1830s- sheep were walked here from as far away as St. Louis

Karl was born in the area and hunted ducks here with his father in the 1920s. In 1923 the prairie was purchased by a real estate company and platted for single family houses. Street beds, which can still be seen, were prepared, and all but sixty acres were sold to separate lot owners. When it came time to put in sewers, the city found that it was impossible because there was a layer of quicksand under the soil.

As on other prairies, occasional fires swept the area, and this aided in preserving the health of the 230 different kinds of plants found on the Markham Prairie, including all of the major tallgrasses, blazing star, and the extremely rare thismia orchid. Efforts to preserve Markham as a natural area began in 1955, and at that time the real estate company donated its remaining sixty acres. It was necessary to purchase the rest of the land from each individual owner with the help of the Nature Conservancy. In 1972 Karl and local Boy Scouts directed a cleanup effort. Fourteen truckloads of trash were removed.

Karl remembers the early fight to preserve Markham Prairie. He tells us: "Local florists used to come in here and take away the wildflowers by the armload. When I would ask them to donate money for its preservation, they would say 'why should we pay for something that is free?'."

The Long Quest

Near the end of September it is time for the fourth annual Save the Tallgrass Prairie Conference. It is held smack in the middle of the Flint Hills at Camp Wood, a YMCA camp at Elmdale, Kansas. In times past, the conference has been a gathering of the best prairie minds rubbing shoulders with environmentalists, bird watchers, little-old-ladies-in-tennis-shoes, students, teachers, a rare politician, and just plain people. It has always been a weekend of learning and fellowship, a general buoying of spirits during the long and frustrating fight to preserve a piece of tallgrass prairie.

I drive down to Camp Wood on Friday night in time to hear my son David play his guitar and sing folk songs for the incoming registrants. The next morning I am too cozy in my sleeping bag to attend the featured prairie bird walk, but I manage to get to the dining hall in time for breakfast. The hall is packed with 300 people, many old friends, from as far away as both coasts. It is a time of warm reunion.

The first speaker of the conference day, after the usual greetings and welcomes, is the lone active Kansas Congressional supporter of the prairie national park, Congressman Larry Winn, Jr. We had been awaiting his reading of H.R. 9120, his new bill introduced into the House of Representatives the previous week. The bill begins:

Be it enacted by the Senate and House of Representatives of the United States of America in Congress assembled, That in recognition of the influence of grasslands, and particularly the

The "godfather" of Markham Prairie is Karl Bartel.

Schwamberger Prairie also is covered with native wild blueberries and strawberries, once a great source of food for the Indians, big and little bluestem, indiangrass, and many other kinds of plants.

tallgrass prairie, upon the progress and economic development of our country, and to preserve the scenic, scientific and educational values of a representative portion of such lands, to preserve the scenery, native plantlife, and native wildlife therein and to provide for the enjoyment of the same in such manner and by such means as will leave them unimpaired for the enjoyment of this and future generations, there is hereby authorized to be established in the manner hereinafter provided the Tallgrass Prairie National Park (Natural Area Category) and the Tallgrass Prairie National Preserve.

Congressman Winn, by his constant support of prairie preservation, is writing a chapter in the history of our country. At this writing there are 19 congressional co-sponsors from all over the country. This new bill calls for a 187,500-acre park and preserve at the Chase South site, a little less than one percent of the total grassland in Kansas, with straighter boundaries than that described in the park service directive of 1975. It differs from all the earlier congressional prairie park bills in that 58 percent of the designated area would be park and 42 percent would be a national preserve (see map). The preserve is so designed as to allow oil and gas extraction until the time that these resources are exhausted. Thereafter the protection afforded the preserve will be indistinguishable from that which the park receives. National preserves closely resemble national parks in management and objectives, but they have less protection in that several kinds of uses may be permitted. The Big Thicket in Texas and the Big Cypress Preserve in Florida are examples of the preserve concept.

H.R. 9120 tries to neutralize major points of opposition to the park by allowing a landowner living within the boundaries of the park or preserve to continue to reside in his or her home for twenty-five years or until the death of the owner or his or her spouse, the choice to be made by the owner. Landowners will also get fair market value when they decide to sell their land to the government. Should the owner reinvest in like property within two years, capital gains will not have to be reported until the reinvestment property is sold, which may be many years, perhaps many generations, in the future. The National Park Service, unlike other government agencies, wants to work only with willing sellers. The power of eminent domain is seldom used and then only as a very last resort.

H.R. 9120 authorizes payments to local governments in lieu of the taxes which would be lost by the lands in the park/preserve. This provision, answering a major objection to the park, cannot be weakened or deleted by anyone as it is a separate public law (94-565) passed by Congress in 1976.

As I listen to Congressman Winn read and explain the bill and speak of his long time support of prairie preservation, I begin to reflect on my own involvement in the political side of this issue. I have never been able to agree with those artists or photographers or any others for that matter who feel that politics is for one reason or another outside their scope of concern. There is no use being an artist if the prime source of inspiration, the natural landscape, is lost. And you can't save the landscape without political involvement. It's uncomfortable, it's work, it's hanging onto a tiger's tail, but it has got to be as much a part of life in a democracy as brushing one's teeth.

My very first contact with this issue was a 1970 feature article in the *Kansas City Star* about Professor E. Raymond Hall, mentioned earlier, the "grand old man" of the park idea in Kansas. After reading the article, there was nothing else to do but go to meet the professor in person at his office on campus. Born in eastern Kansas in 1902, Dr. Hall, author of 334 articles and five, going on six, books, is considered one of a handful of top mammalogists in the world. One of his many continuing activities is attending meetings of the prestigious National Park Service Advisory Board, having been appointed to it by President Eisenhower.

"Where can I see this tallgrass you speak about so lovingly?" I ask. Almost from that moment a warm and lasting friendship developed with this crusty, outspoken, brilliant, amazingly soft, and considerate gentleman, this everlasting student and lover of all living things. Mary Hall, his wife, a botanist and ornithologist in her own right, is just as close to me. Both have taken me, the complete neophyte, under patient wings, teaching me about the grasses and taking me to photogenic prairies. Meetings and trips with the Halls have changed my life forever.

My thoughts are still in the past as the conference speeches go on. I think of my introduction to two other important gentlemen at this time through Dr. Hall: Larry Wagner and his father, R. C. Wagner. Larry

is the attorney mentioned earlier as a founder of STP and a member of the STP park site selection committee. He has contributed untold hours to making the park a reality, and he is a constant inspiration to everyone working for the park. Larry and his father have an active life-long love affair with the tallgrass prairie and will drive out to the Flint Hills at the drop of a hat. They know the back roads better than anyone.

The fight to create a prairie national park had its beginning in the 1930s with the research of Dr. V. E. Shelford of the University of Illinois. Some of his ideas germinated and spawned a number of federal studies between 1937 and 1953. About forty-six years ago, in the Illinois, "The Prairie State," legislature a state bill was introduced to select and preserve a representative sample of tallgrass prairie. A legislator who supported the bill, arose on the floor and asked where he might find an unplowed prairie as he wanted to see it himself and wanted to show it to his family. No one knew, and a few days later it was discovered that the last suitable tract in the state had just been plowed up. That was the end of a prairie park for the Prairie State.

With the continual prodding of Dr. Hall, the National Park Service in 1960 issued a report surveying twenty-four different grasslands as possible park sites. Eighteen were eliminated for various reasons. The six remaining sites were given further exhaustive study, and the Pottawatomie site near Manhattan, Kansas, was chosen. Bills naming this site were introduced by Senator James Pearson and Congressman Larry

"Until we have preserved for our children the biotic wealth of the prairies, we cannot, in truth, sing a halleluja to civilization, for the vast prairie is close to death."

Winn, both of Kansas. The Kansas legislature enthusiastically supported the park idea and appropriated $100,000 to help purchase park land.

In 1962 Dr. Hall founded the Tallgrass Prairie National Park Natural History Association, and it was incorporated as a non-profit citizens' advisory group patterned after citizens' groups connected with other national parks. One of its founding members was Alf Landon, the 1936 Republican presidential candidate who still resides in Topeka. On-site public hearings were planned with Secretary of the Interior Stewart Udall attending. It seemed to be smooth sailing until Secretary Udall stepped from his army helicopter onto a Flint Hills ranch. Awaiting him was an angry gathering of landowners emphasizing their anti-park stance with the law of the West revived—pointed guns. Unfortunately, essential planning with landowners had been overlooked, and that park plan died.

In July 1963 again with the prodding of Dr. Hall, the park service revived the prairie dream by issuing a four-page color chronology listing significant prairie park events going back seventeen years. In the meantime, a formidable obstacle for the park was materializing. In 1962 Joe Skubitz, from the coal mining country of southeast Kansas, was elected to Congress as Kansas' Fifth District representative. The Chase South park site is in this district. Almost from the beginning, Congressman Skubitz, salty, wisecracking, obdurate, but with a keen interest in Kansas history, favored some kind of park, but it was to be his way

or no way. It was never in the cards that he could or would work with Dr. Hall, or anyone connected with Dr. Hall, on this issue. Here were two strong battering rams, each with his own ideas and area of expertise, and neither willing to give an inch. Dr. Hall simply could not compromise the scientific needs of prairie flora and fauna.

The interest was still alive, if just barely, during the turbulence of the 1960s. In 1967 at the time of rising national environmental awareness, Professor Hugh H. Iltis of the University of Wisconsin spoke at the Agriculture Convocation at Kansas State University. In his moving talk "A Requiem for the Prairie" he stated that "until we have preserved for our children the biotic wealth of the prairies, we cannot, in truth, sing a halleluja to civilization, for the vast prairie is close to death."

In 1971 Kansas Governor Robert Docking's Prairie Park Advisory Committee, armed with thousands of supporting letters from Kansans, lobbied in Washington, and this resulted in new bills again sponsored by Senator Pearson and Congressman Winn. These bills, under the guidance of Larry Wagner and Dr. Hall, called for a park of 60,000 acres in the Flint Hills but did not name a specific site. Knowing well the very minimum long-term needs of healthy prairie mammals and birds, Dr. Hall had specific reasons for asking for this size park. Other prairie scientists chided him at the time for not asking for 1,000,000 acres or more considering the enormous size of the original prairie. But Congressman Skubitz, caught in the middle between pro- and anti-park contenders, was up in

We stop one or two more times for pictures of the distinctive stone architecture of the Flint Hills.

arms and called 60,000 acres "unreasonable." By now, he had become the ranking majority member of the House Subcommittee for Parks and Recreation, the subcommittee through which all new park bills must pass before going on to the full Committee for Interior and Insular Affairs, and thence to the floor of the House of Representatives.

Congressman Skubitz was now intractable and actively laying roadblocks for Dr. Hall, Congressman Winn, the growing number of park advocates, and the park service. Because of his position on the subcommittee, his tactics were completely successful. A strong expression of my own developing interest in the park to Congressman Skubitz resulted in a six-page answering tirade the likes of which I had never seen. I was dubbed a "female Moses" because I had the audacity to be an organizer of citizen park support; and I was a woman at that. I was naive to think I could win a war of words with this congressman. From the perspective now of quite a few years, I can smile, but at the time a rage was building within me from the knowledge that one man in Congress could have the power to stop so important a national issue. I made a vow to myself to stay in the fight and win it.

During this time, Congressman Skubitz began to draft his own bill to commemorate the Cherokee Strip, emphasizing local historical events, early day cattle trails, and places where well-known persons lived. He outlined his plan for this park in a 1973 letter to constituents. It was to include some tallgrass prairie but not the required minimum 60,000 acres in one piece. It seemed a good attempt at a compromise. Perhaps we had been wrong after all. Was Skubitz now willing to be the leader we knew he could be and would he work with us? Although wary that our park might get lost in the shuffle, we put out new feelers toward him by announcing publicly our support of his bill. Congressman Winn endorsed the Skubitz proposal in his own press release, making clear that he would still try for 60,000 acres. Winn and several STP members met with Congressman Skubitz, but it became more and more evident that the distance between the two positions had not diminished.

The pro-park people, under the leadership of Dr. Hall and Larry Wagner, were now incorporated as Save the Tallgrass Prairie, Inc., a national, active political lobbying group with a board of directors representing every congressional district in Kansas and members in forty-three states. Charles Stough, a Lawrence, Kansas lawyer and former Speaker of the Kansas House, was elected president of STP, a position which he still holds. In representing the tallgrass prairie throughout the nation, he has gained the love and respect of many people. A national honorary board was appointed with Dr. Karl Menninger as chairman.

Somehow, we believed we must dispel the unfavorable propaganda that was circulating against the park and the park service. STP began disseminating position papers giving well-researched answers to each and every objection, factual or rumor, to the park. A speaker's bureau was organized; a film and slide show were produced; and an information office was staffed with volunteers under the energetic direction of executive vice-president Elaine Shea of Overland Park, Kansas. Chapters of STP were formed in Hays, Wichita, Manhattan, Parsons, and Atchison, Kansas. Mail began pouring in as STP gained national publicity on radio, TV, and in books, newspapers, and periodicals. In 1973 Ray Heady, outdoor editor of the *Kansas City Star*, wrote: "There is a small, hard core group of Kansans who are incorporated as Save the Tallgrass Prairie, Inc., who will never let the idea of a prairie park die. Burn them at the stake, draw and quarter them, bury them under the sod, they will keep right on pushing for a prairie park through their progeny which are many. They simply won't quit. They are sincere, dedicated, knowledgeable and at times mystical in their reverence for the prairie."

Some of the landowners are also sincere in their objections to the park, especially after hearing only one side. They honestly think of STP as a threat to home and livelihood, and they, too, have formed a group to oppose the park called the Grassroots Association. Some members of Grassroots have attended STP meetings and conferences and, although there are still disagreements, they have begun to realize that their real enemy is not the prairie park but insidious land-eating forces over which they have no control. It is to be hoped that the two groups *can* find a way to sit down and work out a good plan for preservation that will be beneficial to all. In April, 1978, a prairie preservation symposium, spon-

sored by Ottawa University at Ottawa, Kansas, was held at the university. On the same platform were STP people and Grassroots members explaining their respective positions. Perhaps this is a beginning.

Certainly, STP should be more vigorous in obtaining the cooperation and good will of landowners and tenants in the vicinity of the park. Richard Pough admonished STP at a previous conference, "It is absolutely essential that you find out who owns every acre of this land and have a frank talk with them." The landowners, too, should realize that as the Flint Hills once passed from government to private ownership, the time has come now to return a tiny fraction

We take a quick look at Alma, another favorite tallgrass prairie town boasting a handsome main street.

to the American people as part of our heritage. STP has always preferred that all but the park area remain privately owned by responsible cattlemen and farmers.

With the popularity of the Flint Hills increasing, many ranches have been repeatedly invaded by well-meaning curiosity-seekers, campers, not-so-well-meaning coyote hunters, and just plain intruders. These "guests" have damaged fences, left cattle gates open, set fires, and generally escalated the already high cost of operating a cattle ranch. It seems that this situation emphasizes the need for a prairie national park. I visualize an unobtrusive park visitor center, perhaps to be manned by local residents, that would dispense attractive educational material describing not only the pre-white man virgin prairie, but also the workings of a modern cattle ranch. The bufferland around the park could contain a demonstration ranch with visitor observation points. Special public events could be built around spring burns, spring roundups, and fall cattle drives. The ever curious public will thus be siphoned from private land and might gain new respect for the landowner.

STP members make trips to Washington. One trip in 1974 resulted in six of the seven Kansas congressional members signing a letter requesting that Secretary of the Interior Rogers C. B. Morton direct the park service to conduct a feasibility study which resulted in the 1975 planning directive. Skubitz refused to sign the request and was successful in blocking even the study for a time. STP also spawned a student automobile caravan to Washington carrying 18,500 signatures of Kansans asking for the park. At this time STP gained the endorsement of all leading national environmental organizations such as the Sierra Club, National Audubon Society, the Izaak Walton League, the Friends of the Earth, and the National Parks and Conservation Association. Other national organizations such as the prestigious American Institute of Architects voted to endorse the park concept. At this writing, all of the Kansas congressional delegation remains publicly uncommitted with the exception of Congressman Winn, but there are signs that this is changing.

There is fresh hope in 1978. Congressman Skubitz has announced his retirement. In 1973 he had stated that the history of the fight for the park has caused him "to believe that a park will be created if not this year, then next year, and almost certainly when I am no longer a member of the National Parks Committee." By delaying the park, he has served as a catalyst for pro-park people to study and to present better bills. H.R. 9120 is the best of all. But the time of the prairie is at hand. The park should be delayed no longer. With the advent of the Carter administration there is "new blood" within the Interior Department working to make the prairie park a high priority item.

I am jolted from my long reflection by loud applause for one of the speakers. Charles Stough, STP president, continues the conference and introduces the next speaker, Dr. Karl Menninger, internationally known psychiatrist, chairman of the honorary board of STP, and the man who "made it easy for us to go out into the

That evening, after all the speeches, panels, workshops, and field trips, I seek a quiet moment on a nearby hillside to try to digest it all. The sun is sending out blades of orange, gold, and blue green reflections between layers of feathery clouds. It is a good sunset and a good omen.

marketplace nationally and secure people whose names have given impetus to the cause such as Loren Eisely, Thomas Hart Benton, Franklin Murphy, and Margaret Mead. While Dr. Karl is coming to the podium I think there is another occasion for a standing ovation."

Dr. Karl's enormous eighty-five-year-old frame, weakened by a recent serious illness, still goes unaided down the middle aisle between the assembled conferees. He begins: "What appeals to Mrs. Menninger and me about this project is that we are not asking for anything . . . we are not trying to gain something for ourselves, we are trying to give something. We are trying to offer millions of people that are alive and to millions that haven't been born yet a beautiful experience." The talk is one we will not soon forget.

That evening, after all the speeches, panels, workshops, and field trips, I seek a quiet moment on a nearby hillside to try to digest it all. The sun is sending out blades

As the cattle come in, they are whooshed into muddy pens, counted, and weighed in fifteen at a time. "Hey, hup," whistles, pounding hooves, and clangs of gates are heard. It is hard, dirty work, but somehow I know that the cowboys would not trade jobs with anyone.

of orange, gold, and blue green reflections between layers of feathery clouds. It is a good sunset and a good omen.

The next day I drive back toward Kansas City with Linda Billings, the Sierra Club representative who had come to the conference from Washington, D.C. We take a small detour and drive north on the prairie parkway to make a quick stop at the Konza. The grass is deep red here and very tall due to the heavy summer rains. We stop one or two more times for pictures of the distinc-

tive stone architecture of the Flint Hills. We pass by the property of one oilman-rancher, the owner of many thousands of acres of tallgrass prairie, a self-styled I-can-do-what-I-damn-well-please-to-*my*-land type of person. This man has plowed up some 6,000 acres of prime Flint Hills native grassland and has replanted it in fescue, giving lie to the myth that in late twentieth century America, the Flint Hills are too rocky to be plowed and that *all* owners will protect the land. We take a quick look at

Alma, another favorite tallgrass prairie town boasting a handsome main street. We arrive at Kansas City International Airport just in time for Linda's plane.

Cattle Drive

Early in October I receive a call from Larry Wagner asking me to accompany him and his dad to the old Spring Hill Ranch fall cattle drive. The ranch is on the prairie parkway north of Strong City. We leave before daylight in a drizzling rain as we want to catch the moment when the cowboys come over the hills with their cattle. The misty rain hugs the hills as we arrive, but we manage to station ourselves at the right place at the right time. The mounted cowboys in their traffic-sign-yellow saddle slickers can be seen for an enormous distance. We are parked near ranch headquarters. As the cattle come in, they are whooshed into muddy pens, counted, and weighed in fifteen at a time. "Hey, hup," whistles, pounding hooves, and clangs of gates are heard. It is hard, dirty work, but somehow I know that the cowboys would not trade jobs with anyone. Theirs is the mystic union that has always existed between man, animal, and land; somehow less intact than that of the American Indian, but still intuitively alive. At last the cattle are prodded into yawning cattle trucks for shipment to Illinois to fatten out on corn.

Just one week later I am back on a neighboring ranch at the invitation of Jack Haden, an old-time cowboy I had met at the cattle drive. This time I drive out alone the night before and stay at the Flint Hills Motel in Strong City. I meet Jack and the others well before daylight at the Fox Creek Ranch headquarters. I am again to be a privileged guest with a ringside seat at a prairie happening: this time the bed of a Ford pickup with a bale of hay for a cushion. We take off across the open, roadless, spectacular ranchland and stop at a prearranged spot. The truck driver says to me: "A big part of this country is nothing but cattle. What I'm trying to do is gather them all [cattle] to me. We feed them, see, and they know the horn [of the truck]."

The sun rises from a pink-hazed horizon. It is the perfect of perfect October days. The clumps of cottonwoods are gold, the grasses are the rainbow of fall colors. The truck is the only sign of civilization. As he honks the horn to gather the cattle, the driver continues: "Way up on that hill, there's a rider there. We got 300 heifers way over there we're going to get." The horn sounds.

On the farthest wave of a hill I can see them. They disappear in a low spot then reappear on another hill. They stay in one cohesive group, much as a flock of ducks or blackbirds fly, moving as if restrained by some invisible placenta. It is a prairie ballet. There are loud and constant horn sounds as the driver tells me more: "These cattle do funny things. Real unpredictable. My wife had some cattle up here. She used to go with me to feed them. We had one called "Old Roamy." She used to feed it by hand. He would watch for her every day. We had one that took mad. He was a miserable old steer. Nowadays we don't have to drive them so far. They got started

The tall, gleaming grain elevators rise out of the prairie at unpredictable intervals. They are the bona fide sculpture of the prairie.

using these pickups to drive these cattle, you know, and it works real good."

The cattle come in and begin to surround the truck. Although the driver has done this thousands of times, there is still excitement in his voice: "There are my little girls! Here they come! All those pretty white faces! Come on little girls! Come on little girls."

There is hot coffee waiting for us when we get back to headquarters. The coffee is as warm and as good as the company.

Breakfast on BlackJack Prairie

In the mail I receive a poster advertising the Maple Leaf Festival at Baldwin City, Kansas :

BREAKFAST ON THE PRAIRIE
BLACKJACK HISTORICAL SOCIETY
Serving sunup to sundown
See SANTA FE TRAIL RUTS
Country Music & Antique Display
Trained Mules

This is too much for me to pass by, so on a crisp Saturday morning Herb and I drive southwest about twenty-five miles on Highway 56, which generally follows the original Santa Fe Trail. BlackJack Prairie, just east of Baldwin City, is a forty-acre tallgrass prairie tract preserved by the Douglas County Historical Society. It is under the gentle, loving guidance of Dr. Ivan Boyd, Professor Emeritus of Botany at nearby Baker University. It is the former site of the village of BlackJack and of what is claimed to be the first skirmish of the Civil War. It seems that in the "Bleeding Kansas" days bands of marauding pro-slav-

ery "ruffians" were constantly crossing the Missouri-Kansas border, raiding, pillaging, and burning free-state settlements. Black-Jack townsmen, forewarned that such a band was coming and with the help of John Brown and three of his sons, made a stand in a grove of blackjack oak trees in the town. The pro-slavery forces surrendered and were taken prisoner. The town no longer exists, but modern citizens have proudly erected a log cabin and a monument and have preserved the prairie remnant complete with the ruts of the old Santa Fe Trail.

We park our car right on the prairie as directed and stand in line for our breakfast of pancakes, sausage, coffee, and cider. There is country music coming from a nearby tent. It is "Darlene and Her Country Cousins," and we step inside out of the wind to enjoy. Darlene sings her own songs of Kansas, sunflowers, and the prairie. Her ear-to-ear grin, like a slice of summer watermelon, captures us. Darlene is absolutely the real thing.

Squaw Creek

The last October trip is to Squaw Creek National Wildlife Refuge, just a two-hour drive north of my home. Squaw Creek, a series of marshy, shallow lakes maintained by the U.S. Fish and Wildlife Service, is in the northwest corner of Missouri near Mound City. Bound by the spectacular loess bluffs, it is a major stopover for migratory waterfowl within the Mississippi flyway. Every spring and fall one can renew one's sense of the Almighty and capture firsthand knowledge of the inviolate

Darlene sings her own songs of Kansas, sunflowers, and the prairie. Her ear-to-ear grin, like a slice of summer watermelon, captures us. Darlene is absolutely the real thing.

Is the prairie a clear answer to a question it takes all of a life to learn to ask?

I'm back home now, and I walk on my Quivira prairie waiting for the first frost, the big change, the shutdown of the year of the prairie.

rhythms of our planet by witnessing the hundreds of thousands of birds and bird sounds which fill the sky from horizon to horizon. It is religion on a grand scale—sights and sounds which can lift you out of yourself and stretch your mind and spirit to oneness with the cosmos. How many thousands of years has the earth nurtured the birds? If man has trouble finding his direction, birds do not.

Death—and Life Again

We've almost lost this inland sea of grass that set the character of a free America. For 125 years we have lost, each and every year, an area ten times the size of that which we want for the national park.

Why cannot we connect human life to prairie life? A civilization that destroys the right-to-life of a coyote eventually destroys my right-to-life. We're equals: coyotes, golden eagles, voles, and human beings. The wild prairie is a celebration of diversity—the law of life on this planet.

The prairie reveals not only its subtle beauty slowly, but also the forces destroying it. It is not lost loudly like the majestic redwoods. Inch by relentless inch, it goes so that even the landowners are fooled. A highway, a reservoir, a new plowed field, a new power plant, a careless tenant, it goes.

The native grasses are decorative, picturesque, superb for controlling erosion, rebuilding soil, cleaning water and air. Prairie grass stores water for drought, crowds out weeds, and holds secrets about new food sources. Prairie soil contains billions of one-celled factories—bacteria—that make fertilizer. Museums, highway rights-of-way, campuses, arboretums, wildlife preserves, airports, industrial sites, and even residential landscapes need to bloom with the vibrant colors of big and little bluestem, indiangrass, switchgrass and the other native grasses.

I'm back home now, and I walk on my Quivira prairie waiting for the first frost, the big change, the shutdown of the year of the prairie. The bright wildflower stalks clutch at me like a last supplicant before taking the veil. Is it always so lovely just before death? Is death really the end, or does it begin another cycle? Is the prairie a clear answer to a question it takes all of a life to learn to ask?

My gentle father reached *his* death this month of October. Was the timing coincidental? I think not. We are not so aimless after all. On the prairie is a wheel for everything: grass, fungi, soil, shrubs, flowers, wind, sky, rain—millions of living things enmeshed, interlocking, turning with the seasons, teaching us. The prairie speaks plainly to man, and we must listen. The prairie is the landscape most related to man and most changed by man. I'd give an arm and a leg to see it as it was.

We didn't talk much, my father and I, during his final illness, but he spoke to me with his eyes. Is it presumptuous of me to say that I understand what he was saying, he who spent his life teaching me and many others about the natural world?

Yes, the prairie was in my blood before I was born. Rachel, my grandmother, saw to that. And it will be there when I die. Right now, I still hop around the landscape trying to drink it all in before it's gone.

MAJOR NATIVE PLANTS AND ANIMALS

GRASSES

Big bluestem
Little bluestem
Indiangrass
Switch grass
Canada wild-rye
Prairie cordgrass or sloughgrass
Side-oats grama
Junegrass or crested hairgrass
Eastern gamagrass
Western wheatgrass
Dropseed
Sand dropseed
Stinkgrass, lovegrass
Purple lovegrass
Purpletop
Little barley
Prairie three-awn grass
Porcupine grass

FLOWERS (in order of bloom)

April-May

Pasqueflower
Pussytoes
Birdsfoot violet
Hoary puccoon
Yellowstar grass
Golden alexander
Wild strawberry
Houstonia
Shooting star
Lousewort
Indian paintbrush
Ground plum
Wild indigo
Purple milkweed
Blue-eyed grass
Prairie anemone
Wild alfalfa
Verbena

Canada anemone
Nuttall's prairie parsley
Carrot-leaved parsley
Daisy fleabane
Western fleabane
Prairie ragwort
Camassia
Flowering spurge
Prairie phlox

June

Common spiderwort
Prairie smoke
Blue false indigo
Cream false indigo
Prairie rose
Ox-eye daisy
Pale spike lobelia
Butterfly milkweed
Blackeyed susan
Coreopsis
Goatsrue
Antelope horn
    (milkweed)
Purple poppy mallow
Lead plant
Prairie white fringed orchid
Wild onion
Prairie turnip
Catsclaw sensitivebriar
Culver's root
Mountain mint
Bunch flower
Pale purple coneflower
    (Blacksampson)
Cobaea penstamen
Dwarf larkspur
Hawkweed
Horseweed fleabane
Hairy ruellia
    (false petunia)

Tuberous Indian plantain
New Jersey tea
False toadflax
Tick trefoil
Canada wild lettuce
Michigan lily

July

Ironweed
Prairie dock
Rattlesnake master
Compass plant
Common milkweed
Prairie blazingstar (gayfeather)
Purple prairie clover
White prairie clover
Evening primrose or
    Missouri primrose
Rosin weed
Western venus looking glass
Swamp milkweed
Vervain
Pinate leaved coneflower

August

Common sunflower
Showy goldenrod
Hairy white aster
Ladies' tresses
Azure aster
Stiff goldenrod
Broomweed
Dotted gayfeather
Pitcher's sage
False boneset
Round headed bush clover
Prairie mimosa
Tall thorowort

September-October

Downy gentian
Bottle gentian

Fringed gentian
Heath aster
Saw-toothed sunflower
Willow leafed sunflower
Cardinal flower
Button snakeroot
White lettuce

MAMMALS

Opossum
Raccoon
Coyote
White-tailed deer
Red fox
Gray fox
Bobcat
Beaver
Muskrat
Woodchuck
Mink
Long-tailed weasel
Least weasel
Striped skunk
Badger
13-Lined ground squirrel
Gray squirrel
Fox squirrel
Chipmunk
Franklin's ground squirrel
Meadow jumping mouse
Deer mouse
White-footed mouse
Meadow vole
Prairie vole
Pine vole
Eastern cottontail
Eastern mole
Least shrew
Short-tailed shrew
Masked shrew
Red bat
Hoary bat

Big brown bat
Little brown bat
Keen's bat
Black-tailed jack rabbit
Woodchuck
Plains pocket gopher
Hispid cotton rat
Wood rat
Porcupine
River otter
Wapiti (elk)
Bison
Armadillo
Prong-horned antelope
Gray wolf
Black bear

BIRDS

Hawk, eastern red-tailed
Owl, great horned
Owl, northern barred
Cardinal, eastern
Hawk, eastern sparrow
Owl, barn
Owl, long-eared
Hawk, Cooper's
Bobwhite
Owl, screech
Robin
Nighthawk
Oriole, orchard
Tanager, scarlet
Tanager, summer
Thrasher, brown
Thrasher, wood
Towhee, red-eyed
Tanager, scarlet
Grosbeak, rosebreasted
Hummingbird, rubythroated
Redstart, American
Sparrow, eastern lark
Swallow, barn

Wren, Carolina
Wren, Texas
Wren, western house
Hawk, ferrugenous rough-legged
Hawk, marsh
Hawk, sharp-shinned
Hawk, red-tailed
Dove, mourning
Longspur, chestnut-collared
Longspur, Lapland
Longspur, Smith's
Sparrow, eastern fox
Sparrow, song
Bittern, American
Mallard, common
Canvasback
Merganser, American
Shoveller
Bittern, eastern least
Rail, king
Teal, blue-winged
Duck, ruddy
Teal, green-winged
Red-wing, eastern
Red-wing, giant
Sandpiper, eastern solitary
Sandpiper, least
Crow, eastern
Heron, great blue
Vulture, turkey
Kite, Mississippi
Bluebird, eastern
Jay, northern blue
Starling
Woodpecker, redheaded
Woodpecker, eastern hairy
Woodpecker, red-bellied
Catbird
Chuck-will's-widow
Cowbird, eastern
Kingbird, Arkansas
Kingbird, eastern

Martin, purple
Mockingbird
Whip-poor-will
Thrush, gray-cheeked
Thrush, olive-backed
Chickadee, blackcapped
Nuthatch, white-breasted
Titmouse, tufted
Bunting, indigo
Pewee, eastern wood
Phoebe, eastern
Sparrow, eastern chipping
Sparrow, western grasshopper
Swallow, cliff
Swift, chimney
Creeper, brown
Junco, slatecolored
Sparrow, eastern tree
Sparrow, Harris's
Flycatcher, least
Flycatcher, scissor-tailed
Sparrow, clay-colored
Sparrow, eastern vesper
Sparrow, Lincoln's
Sparrow, Savannah
Sparrow, white-crowned
Swallow, tree
Warbler, black and white
Warbler, black-poll
Bluebird, eastern
Meadowlark
Blackbird, redwing
Shrike, migrant
Lark, horned
Dickcissel
Heron, yellow-crowned night
Heron, black-crowned night
Baldpate
Goose, common Canada
Goose, Hutchin's
Coot, American
Killdeer

Kingfisher, eastern belted
Goldfinch, eastern
Egret, American
Pelican, white
Prairie chicken, greater

PRAIRIE INFORMATION SOURCES

BOERNER BOTANICAL GARDENS
Whitnall Park
Hales Corners, Wisconsin 53130
Experimental restored tallgrass prairie,
educational material.

LAFAYETTE HOME NURSERY, INC.
Ingels Brothers
LaFayette, Illinois 61449
Establishing prairies since 1887.

MIDWEST PRAIRIE BIENNIAL CONFERENCES
c/o Dr. Lloyd Hulbert
Division of Biology
Kansas State University
Manhattan, Kansas 66502
Conferences held at various prairie
universities every two years.

THE MISSOURI PRAIRIE FOUNDATION
P.O. Box 200
Columbia, Missouri 65201
Acquires land for preservation in Missouri.

THE NATURE CONSERVANCY
Patrick Noonan, President
1800 North Kent Street
Arlington, Virginia 22209
Effort to find and conserve virgin prairies.

PLANT MATERIALS CENTER—USDA
Rt. 2
Manhattan, Kansas 66502
Native prairie flora research.

PRAIRIE RESTORATIONS, INC.
Ron Bowen
807 South Third Street
Princeton, Minnesota 55371
Wildflower and native grass seeds
and seedlings; prairie management;
plans restoration sites.

SAVE THE TALLGRASS PRAIRIE, INC.
Elaine Shea, Executive Vice President
4101 West 54th Terrace
Shawnee Mission, Kansas 66205
Educational and political information.

SOIL CONSERVATION SOCIETY OF AMERICA
7515 N.E. Ankeny Road
Ankeny, Iowa 50021
Dispenses educational material.

STOCK SEED FARMS
Route 1, Box 112
Murdock, Nebraska 68407
Prairie grasses for lawns and landscaping.

THE TALLGRASS PRAIRIE FOUNDATION
5450 Buena Vista
Shawnee Mission, Kansas 66205
Acquires land for preservation, dispenses
educational material.

WINDRIFT PRAIRIE SHOP
Douglas E. Wade
R. D. 2
Oregon, Illinois 61061
Prairie books, art prints and seeds.

BIBLIOGRAPHY

Aldrich, Bess Streeter. *The Rim of the Prairie.* Lincoln: University of Nebraska, 1925.

Allen, Durward L. *The Life of Prairies and Plains.* New York: McGraw-Hill, 1967.

Angle, Paul M., ed. *Prairie State: Impressions of Illinois, 1673-1967, by Travelers and Other Observers.* Chicago: University of Chicago Press, 1968.

Arese, Francesco. *A Trip to the Prairies in the Interior of the Interior of North America.* Translated by Andrew Evans. New York: The Harbor Press, 1837-38.

Atkinson, J. Brooks. *This Bright Land.* New York: Doubleday, 1971.

Barns, Cass G. *The Sod House.* Lincoln: University of Nebraska, 1930

Barry, Louise. *The Beginning of the West. Annals of the Kansas Gateway to the American West, 1540-1854.* Topeka: Kansas Historical Society, 1972.

Betz, Robert F. *Prairie Plants of the Chicago Region.* Lisle, Illinois: The Morton Arboretum, 1965.

Billard, Jules B., ed. *The World of the American Indian.* Washington, D.C.: National Geographic Society, 1974.

Boerner, Alfred L. *Prairie Propagation Handbook.* Hales Corners, Wisconsin: Boerner Botanical Garden, Whitnall Park, 1972.

Brown, Mark H. and Felton, W. R. *The Frontier Years: L. A. Huffman, Photographer of the Plains.* New York: Henry Holt & Company, 1955.

Brown, William E. *Islands of Hope—Parks and Recreation in Environmental Crises.* Washington, D.C.: National Parks and Recreation Association, 1971.

Bull, John and Farrand, John, Jr. *The Audubon Society Field Guide to North American Birds, Eastern Region.* New York: Alfred A. Knopf, 1977.

Carson, Rachel. *The Sense of Wonder.* New York: Harper and Row, 1956.

Cather, Willa. *My Antonia.* 1918. Reprint. New York: Houghton Miflin Co., 1954.

Catlin, George. *Letters and Notes on the North American Indians.* Edited by Michael M. Mooney. New York: Clarkson N. Potter, Inc., 1975.

Coats, Alice. *The Plant Hunters.* New York: McGraw-Hill, 1970.

Cooper, J. Fennimore. *The Prairie.* 1827. Reprint. New York: Dodd, Mead, 1954.

Costello, David F. *The Prairie World.* New York: Thomas Y. Crowell Co., 1969.

Custer, Elizabeth Bacon. *Tenting on the Plains.* Norman: University of Oklahoma Press, 1971.

Dary, David. *The Buffalo Book.* Chicago: The Swallow Press, Inc., 1974.

Denison, Edgar. *Missouri Wildflowers.* Missouri Department of Conservation, 1973.

Dillard, Annie. *Pilgrim at Tinker Creek.* New York: Harper & Row, 1974.

Francois des Montaignes. *The Plains.* Edited by Nancy A. Mower and Don Russell. Norman: University of Oklahoma Press, 1972.

Franzwa, Gregory M. *The Oregon Trail Revisited.* St. Louis: Patrice Press, Inc., 1972.

Fremont, John Charles. *The Exploring Expedition to the Rocky Mountains, Oregon and California.* Buffalo: George H. Derby and Co., 1851.

Frome, Michael. *The National Parks.* Chicago: Rand McNally, 1977.

Gladstone, T. H. *The Englishman in Kansas.* 1857. Reprint. Lincoln: University of Nebraska, 1971.

Gregg, Josiah. *Commerce of the Prairies.* Edited by Max L. Moorhead. Norman: University of Oklahoma, 1954.

Gregg, Kate L. *The Road to Santa Fe. The Journal and Diaries of George Champlin Sibley.* Albuquerque: University of New Mexico Press, 1975.

Grossman, Mary Louise. *Our Vanishing Wilderness.* New York: Grossett and Dunlap, 1969.

Hall, E. Raymond. *Handbook of Mammals of Kansas.* State Biological Survey of Kansas, misc. Pub. No. 7. Lawrence: University of Kansas Press, 1955.

Harris, Edward. *Up the Missouri with Audubon, The Journal of Edward Harris.* Edited by John Francis McDermott. Norman: University of Oklahoma, 1951.

Irving, Washington. *A Tour on the Prairies.* Reprint. 1832. Norman: University of Oklahoma, 1954.

Ise, John. *Sod and Stubble*. Lincoln: University of Nebraska, 1936.

Killoren, Robert. *Rising Out of the Flint Hills*. Shawnee Mission, Kansas: Bookmark Press, 1972.

Korling, Torkel. *The Prairie Swell and Swale*. Dundee, Illinois, 1972.

Leopold, Aldo. *A Sand County Almanac*. New York: Ballantine Books, 1970.

Lewis and Clark. *History of the Expedition Under the Command of Lewis and Clark*. Edited by Elliott Coues, 3 vols. Reprint. New York: Dover Publications, 1965.

Mathews, John Joseph. *The Osages*. Norman: University of Oklahoma, 1961.

McCarter, Margaret Hill. *The Price of the Prairie*. New York: A. L. Burt Co., 1910.

McLuhan, T. C. *Touch the Earth*. New York: Outerbridge and Dienstfrey, 1971.

Michener, James A. *Centennial*. New York: Random House, 1974.

Miller, Nyle H. *Great Gunfighters of Kansas Cowtowns, 1867-1886*. Lincoln: University of Nebraska, 1963.

_____. *Pasture and Range Plants*. Bartlesville, Oklahoma: Phillips Petroleum Company, 1963.

Neihardt, John G. *Black Elk Speaks*. Lincoln: University of Nebraska Press, 1961.

Peattie, Donald Culross. *A Prairie Grove*. New York: Simon and Schuster, Inc., 1938.

Plowden, David. *The Floor of the Sky: The Great Plains*. San Francisco: Sierra Club, 1972.

Proposed Prairie National Park. Kansas/Oklahoma Planning Directive. Washington, D.C.: U.S. Department of the Interior National Park Service, 1975.

Richmond, Robert W. *Kansas: A Land of Contrasts*. St. Charles, Missouri: Forum Press, 1974.

Rolvaag, Ole Edvart. *Giants in the Earth: A Saga of the Prairie*. 1927. Reprint. New York: Harper & Row, 1967.

Rydberg, Per Axel. *Flora of the Prairies and Plains of Central North America*. 2 vols. New York: Dover Publications, 1971.

Sandburg, Carl. *Cornhuskers*. New York: Holt and Company, 1918.

Sandoz, Mari. *Love Song to the Plains*. Lincoln: University of Nebraska Press, 1961.

Savage, William, ed. *Cowboy Life: Reconstructing An American Myth*. Norman: University of Oklahoma Press, 1975.

Schwartz, Charles W. *The Prairie Chicken*. Jefferson City, Missouri, 1944.

Shea, Elaine, ed. *Saving the Prairie Two Days at a Time*. Save the Tallgrass Prairie, Inc. Shawnee Mission, Kansas, 1974.

Socolofsky, Homer E. *The Historical Atlas of Kansas*. Norman: University of Oklahoma, 1972.

Stout, Mel J. *A Proposed Tallgrass Prairie National Park*. Lansing: University of Michigan, 1972.

The Old West. Little-Life Books. 20 vols. Hedley Donovan, Editor-in-Chief. Alexandria, Virginia, 1977.

Tixier, Victor. *Travels on the Osage Prairies*. Edited by John Francis McDermott. Norman: University of Oklahoma.

Udall, Stewart L. *The Quiet Crises*. New York: Avon Books, 1963.

Viola, Herman J. *The Indian Legacy of Charles Bird King*. Washington, D.C.: Smithsonian Institution Press, 1976.

Wagner, Henry. *The Plains and Rockies: A Bibliography of Original Narratives of Travel and Adventure 1800-1865*. San Francisco: J. Howell, 1921.

Walton, George. *Sentinel of the Plains: Fort Leavenworth and the American West*. Englewood Cliffs, New Jersey: Prentice-Hall, Inc. 1973.

Weaver, J. E. *North American Prairies*. Lincoln: University of Nebraska Press, 1954.

_____. *Prairie Plants and Their Environment*. Lincoln: University of Nebraska Press, 1958.

Webb, Walter Prescott. *The Great Plains*. New York: Ginn and Company, 1931.

Wilder, Laura Ingalls. *Little House on the Prairie*. Reprint. New York: Harper & Row, 1971.

_____. *By the Shores of Silver Lake*. Reprint. New York: Harper & Row, 1971.

Wilson, Jim and Alice. *Grassland*. Polk, Nebraska: Wide Skies Press, 1967.

Zimmerman, James H. *Proceedings of the Second Midwest Prairie Conference*. Madison: University of Wisconsin, 1972.

INDEX

112

PHOTOGRAPHS